The Book of Blessings

Impacting Lives with the Language of God

R. Scott Osborne
FOREWORD BY DR. SAMUEL FARINA

Copyright © 2007 by R. Scott Osborne

The Book of Blessings by R. Scott Osborne

Printed in the United States of America

ISBN 978-1-60266-744-0

All rights reserved solely by the author. The author guarantees all contents are original and do not infringe upon the legal rights of any other person or work. No part of this book may be reproduced in any form without the permission of the author. The views expressed in this book are not necessarily those of the publisher.

Unless otherwise indicated, Bible quotations are taken from The King James Version of the Holy Bible (also known as the Authorized Version). This translation of the Holy Bible is in the Public Domain.

Scripture quotations marked "CJB" are taken from the *Complete Jewish Bible*, copyright © 1998 by David H. Stern. Published by Jewish New Testament Publications, Inc. www.messianicjewish.net/jntp. Distributed by Messianic Jewish Resources. www.messianicjewish.net. All rights reserved. Used by permission.

Quotations marked "KJV" are taken from The King James Version of the Holy Bible (also known as the Authorized Version). This translation of the Holy Bible is in the Public Domain.

Scripture quotations marked "NASB" are taken from the New American Standard Bible®, Copyright © 1960, 1962, 1963, 1968, 1971, 1972, 1973, 1975, 1977, 1995 by The Lockman Foundation. Used by permission (www.Lockman.org)

Scripture quotations marked "NCV" are taken from the New Century Version®. Copyright © 2005 by Thomas Nelson, Inc. Used by permission. All rights reserved.

Scripture quotations marked "NIV" are taken from the HOLY BIBLE, NEW INTERNATIONAL VERSION®. NIV®. Copyright© 1973, 1978, 1984 by International Bible Society. Used by permission of Zondervan. All rights reserved.

Scripture quotations marked "NIrV" are taken from the HOLY BIBLE, NEW INTERNATIONAL READER'S VERSION®. NIV®. Copyright© 1994, 1996 by International Bible Society. Used by permission of Zondervan. All rights reserved.

Scripture quotations marked "NKJV" are taken from the New King James Version®. Copyright © 1982 by Thomas Nelson, Inc. Used by permission. All rights reserved.

Scripture quotations marked "NLT" are taken from the Holy Bible, New Living Translation, copyright © 1996. Used by permission of Tyndale House Publishers, Inc, Wheaton, Illinois 60189. All rights reserved.

Scripture quotations marked "RSV" are taken from the Revised Standard Version of the Bible, copyright 1952 [2nd edition, 1971] by the Division of Christian Education of the National Council of the Churches of Christ in the United States of America. Used by permission. All rights reserved.

Scripture quotations marked "TNIV" are taken from the HOLY BIBLE, TODAY'S NEW INTERNATIONAL VERSION®. TNIV®. Copyright© 2001, 2005 by International Bible Society. Used by permission of Zondervan. All rights reserved.

www.xulonpress.com

To my wife Daryse,
Thank you for your constant love, support and faithfulness. I could not have completed this without you. You are invaluable to me.

To my daughters, Chloe and Hannah,
Thank you for always believing in me.

To my son-in-law Kyle and grandson Klaus,
I am so thankful you are part of my life.

To my mother,
Thank you for my strong Christian heritage and for instilling me with the desire to serve God.

To my heavenly Father,
Thank you for saving us and blessing us with your Word.

I love you all!

Contents

Forward 1
Preface 3
Introduction 7
    Clarification on Use of Specific Scriptures 10
    Format 11
1   The Positive & Negative
    Effect of Words 13
    Affirmation and a Whole Lot More 14
    The "Anti-" Blessing 15
    No Middle Ground 16
2   The Blessing 19
    What is a Blessing? 20
    How to Bless – The Model Blessing 22
    Why We Bless – Our Priestly Duty 26
    Transformed by the Word 29
    Heart Surgery 32
3   Imparting Blessings 33
    When and Whom to Bless 33
    Constructing a Blessing 33
    How to Use this Book 35
    Two Unique Categories 37
    Laying on of Hands 38
    Go and Do Thou Likewise 39
4   Blessings about Redemption & Restoration 41
5   Blessings for God's Abiding Presence 47
6   Blessings about God's Word 53
7   Blessings for God's Favor 57
8   Blessings for God's Guidance 63
9   Blessings for God's Mercy,
    Grace, & Compassion 67
10 Blessings for God's Protection & Safety 71
11 Blessings for God's Provision 79
12 Blessings over Family 85
13 Blessings for God's Children 91

14	Blessings about Confrontation	95
15	Blessings for Courage	101
16	Blessings about Destiny & Calling	107
17	Blessings for Encouragement	111
18	Blessings for Godly Character	115
19	Blessings for Godly Speech	125
20	Blessings for Healing & Long Life	129
21	Blessings for Joy	133
22	Blessings for Anointing in Ministry	139
23	Blessings for Peace, Rest & Patience	147
24	Blessings for Faith & Trust	153
25	Blessings for Wisdom, Knowledge & Discernment	157
26	Blessings to God	163
27	Blessings over Israel	169

Appendix A 185
Israel & the Church 185
    The Abrahamic Covenant 185
    The Covenant Ritual 186
    God Remembered 187
    An Unconditional Covenant 188
    For the Sake of His Name 189
    Enter, the Church 191
    One Body 192

Appendix B 195
Biblical Examples of Blessings 195
    Blessings By God the Father 195
    Blessings by Old Testament "Visitors" 197
    Blessings by Jesus, God the Son 198
    Blessings by the Saints of Scripture 199

The Book of Blessings Website 211

Forward

I have been a pastor of the same congregation for over forty years. Through all those years I have concluded the services with the priestly benediction from Numbers 6, "The Lord bless thee, and keep thee: The Lord make His face to shine upon thee, and be gracious unto thee: The Lord lift up His countenance upon thee, and give thee peace" (KJV). I would then add spontaneous blessings usually pertaining to the burden of the message I had preached.

Though I did not fully realize the power of these blessings, people took the benediction seriously and began to expect that blessings would be pronounced over them. As the years passed, it put me to thinking, when *did* this practice first touch my life?

It all began with my parents – faithfully speaking blessings over my siblings and me. That's one of the reasons all six of the Farina children have served the Lord and four of us have been pastors for many years. I also recall my childhood Pastor, Silvio Marcadonna, who would regularly lay hands on me and pronounce blessing in his Italian immigrant accent, "The Lord is going to use you, Samuel!" The profound truth is that my palate for blessing was touched from the earliest point of my upbringing.

In the early years of my ministry I continued to seek out godly men to lay hands on me and bless me – men like Elder Karl F. Smith, Ern Baxter, Judson Cornwall and others. Each one impacted my life and ministry in a particular way. Do I believe in the power of blessing? I certainly do.

I'm excited to recommend this book to you because I have witnessed the impact of blessings on the lives of others. My own life has been greatly impacted by the spoken blessing. Because others were obedient to the voice of the Lord, they expressed blessings over me. If we will allow the Holy Spirit to guide us, we will all become speakers of blessing. It is God's way.

The Book of Blessings, compiled by my spiritual son, Scott Osborne, is a book to include in your spiritual arsenal – a book to use to bless others and to receive blessing. This book stands unique among the volumes that have been written about blessings because it amasses literally hundreds of Scriptures with which to bless. This matters because the God we serve is the Author of all blessing. He alone is the Source of blessing and His Word is a vital resource for which there is no substitute. Nothing encourages, nothing soothes, and nothing breathes hope like the Word of God.

As we bless with the Holy Scriptures, we are able to sow the Living Word into the lives of others in order to bring God's blessing upon them and facilitate their transformation into His image. May we generously speak blessings so that we might all become instruments of affirmation in God's hands.

Dr. Samuel Farina

May 8, 2007

Preface

There are many ways to characterize passages of Scripture. Some Scriptures are laws, some are prophesies, some are songs of praise or worship, some are prayers, some are poetry, and some narrate Biblical history. But there are also blessings. There are recorded acts of God's powers and there are sobering passages revealing God's hand of judgment. And there are the blessings of God. The Scripture is threaded with the saga of man's greed, lust, and quest for power. But there are inspiring accounts of godly men and women who share the love of God by blessing their fellow man. Nearly every time I read the Scriptures, I see blessings.

This book is a product of my personal experience…an experience shared by my entire family. It began in 1988, when we joined a church named Christian Assembly in Columbus, Ohio and came under the pastorate of Doctor Samuel Farina. Among his many life-impacting practices is his speaking of blessings over the congregation. Pastor Sam imparts a blessing over a group or an individual as instinctively as sharing a hug or a prayer. Our pastor set the example for my family and opened our eyes to a lifestyle of blessing.

Fast forward about twelve years when we were introduced to a Friday night tradition by our dear friends, Carl and Yvonne Peters. As a family, we began a weekly observance of the Sabbath (or "Shabbat," in Hebrew). It has been a delight, as American Christians, to share in this centuries-old Jewish tradition. As in

Jewish homes all over the world, our Shabbat Eve observance begins with the speaking of various blessings. There are blessings spoken to God for the "welcoming" of Shabbat and the lighting of the Shabbat candles, for the drinking of the wine, for the ceremonial washing of hands, and for the eating of the bread.

We also take turns speaking blessings over one another. As parents, we speak over our children, grandchildren, and spiritual children. I speak a blessing over my wife and she speaks a blessing over me. There is also a blessing from our children to us. Shabbat has become a special, sweet time in the life of our family and our "oasis in time" is usually the brightest spot in our week. Thus began the Osborne family practice of speaking blessings to one another.

As time passed, I found myself adding what we eventually called "bonus" blessings during our Shabbat observances. I adapted verses of Scripture into the form of a blessing I felt would be meaningful to my family. They began to anticipate their bonus blessing and before long a new element had been added to our weekly tradition. I believe with all my heart that years of blessing my family significantly contributed to their spiritual and emotional growth in a lasting and meaningful way.

As the Lord continued to show me passage after passage of Scripture containing words of blessing, I began keeping them in a journal. My list of Scriptures grew and I increased my practice of speaking blessings from the Bible to others. Over time, I felt an overwhelming call from God to write a book containing all the blessings. I humbly offer this as my faithful and best effort to fulfill that mission.

My hope is for this book to be used somewhat like a reference book by the reader. It is not a book merely to be read, though I do not discourage anyone from doing so. This book is a resource, intended to be used day after day and week after week by anyone who wants to apply the language of God to impact the lives of others. I hope your copy will reveal significant signs of wear over time.

Let me talk practically about what this book is *not*. It is *not* about some formula for victorious living. Please don't think if you say enough blessings over someone that you are assured of seeing change. Change may occur and blessings will certainly contribute. However, there are so many factors influencing anyone's life, we would be misled to assume that blessings alone can bring about transformation or growth. God operates out of love and grace and we must never think we can obligate Him to bring about *our* expectations.

Neither does this book intend to present itself as a comprehensive treatment of the Biblical teachings on blessing. This book is meant only to establish a basic framework that will motivate readers to begin blessing others. It is designed to quickly launch you into the practice of blessing.

I remind us that we are all directed by God to speak blessings. When we do, we are following the example of God and the great men of the Bible. As we speak God's Word, we convey His influence to the world around us.

We know God and His Word are one, therefore any time we appropriate His Word, we invite His heart and His power into a situation. My prayer is that you will invite God's heart and power into situations involving the people in your life by using His language to speak blessings over them.

> Beloved, I wish above all things
> that thou mayest prosper and be in health,
> even as thy soul prospereth.
> ~ 3 John 1:2 (KJV) ~

Introduction

The blessing of Adonai is what makes people rich,
and He doesn't mix sorrow with it.
~ Proverbs 10:22 (CJB) ~

A blessing may be verbal or nonverbal. A nonverbal blessing might be an act of service, the giving of a gift, or just spending time with someone who enjoys your company. The focus of this book is on the *speaking* of blessings and specifically the speaking of blessings based on Scripture. This is important because the Word of God we call *The Holy Bible* is sacred, infallible, and living. It communicates the very heart, character, and plan of God in words He carefully chose.

If we wish to speak into people's lives with power, love, and anointing, our best opportunity for impact is to recite the Word of God. God's Word is vastly superior to anything we can think or say. Therefore, as we season our speech with His Word, we are equipping ourselves with a sword that truly has the potential to cut to the heart of any matter.

We also want to declare blessings based on the Word because we will be using the *language of God*. When I say the "language of God," I am referring to the expressions and concepts communicated by the Lord through His *words* in His *Word*. What better example could we use to model our own speech than the words, phrases, and word pictures used by our Creator Himself? After all, He is the source of all blessing.

If God uses certain terminology to describe the value of His chosen people, then the beauty of that picture is something I want to mimic in describing the value of those who are dear to me. If God articulated His delight in King David using particular words, then I want to imitate His language in describing my delight in someone special. The Lord uses many terms to describe His awesome powers, His provision, and His love for us. I want to use the same words when I pray for His love and provision or His insertion of power into the life of someone for whom I am interceding. Are you getting the idea?

I doubt this is a new concept for any of us. As practicing believers, we routinely appropriate the Word of God in the course of everyday life. It may be exhorting our children to, "Do unto others as you would have them do unto you." My mother often said, "Love covers a multitude of sins." It isn't uncommon to hear phrases like "an eye for an eye," "turn the other cheek," or "seek and you shall find." We use these expressions because they are relevant to our lives. The Bible is so universal and it applies to so many situations, we eventually all seem to find ourselves quoting from it in ordinary conversation, whether consciously or not. I believe God is pleased when we do this.

This book contains over five hundred Scriptures that have been modified to create blessings. In other words, the language of God was used to phrase each blessing. Although the blessings were extracted from their Biblical context, great care was taken to preserve the essence of each Scripture. The vibrancy of God's Word has been retained, even though the applications may be new. For every blessing in the book, its Scripture reference is provided to facilitate the reader's personal exploration into the original passage from which it came.

Allow me to cite some examples for clarification. The context in chapter one of First Timothy is Paul describing how he was entrusted with the Good News, even though he was the "number one sinner." Despite his history of blasphemy and persecution, he was granted God's grace and forgiveness. Paul continued in verse 14, *"The grace of our Lord was poured out on me abundantly, along with the faith and love that are in Christ Jesus"* (NIV).

This verse also expresses a beautiful truth about God's grace toward all of us who are sinners and have fallen short of the glory of God. I adapted 1 Timothy 1:14 as a blessing in this way, *"May the grace of the Lord pour out on you abundantly, along with the faith and love that are in Christ Jesus."* In doing so, I am able to convey the message of God's mercy and grace to others as I bless them. Though the application has changed, this truth clearly applies to us just as it did to Paul.

Let me provide another example of how a Scripture was customized into the form of a blessing. In 2 Samuel 22:34 (a thanksgiving psalm of David) we read, *"He makes me as surefooted as a deer, leading me safely along the mountain heights"* (NLT). A blessing for God's protection based on this verse reads, *"May God make you as surefooted as a deer, leading you safely along the mountain heights."*

In many cases words are added for amplification. The next example comes from the same passage. 2 Samuel

22:35 reads, *"He trains my hands for battle, so that my arms can bend a bow of bronze"* (NASB). A blessing for courage based on this verse reads, *"May the Lord train your hands for battle, so that your arms can bend a bow of bronze. May He equip you for any challenge or confrontation, that by the strength of Him who is your source, you will be able to do the impossible."*

Clarification on Use of Specific Scriptures

Some readers will notice my occasional use of promises and prophetic Scriptures that God originally intended for the nation of Israel.

First, I confidently use these verses because the promises and prophesies for Israel also apply to us...by way of Israel, not in place of Israel. *"If you belong to Christ, then you are Abraham's seed, and heirs according to the promise"* (Gal. 3:29, NIV). The Apostle Paul also wrote, *"You Gentiles, who were branches from a wild olive tree, were grafted in. So now you also receive the blessing God has promised Abraham and his children, sharing in God's rich nourishment of his special olive tree"* (Rom. 11:17, NLT). Additional discussion on the relationship between Israel and the Church can be found in *Appendix A*.

Secondly – except in the chapter, *Blessings for Israel* – I did not attempt to represent the literal context from which these promises and prophesies are quoted. In all other chapters, I applied the language of God for a blessing with a contemporary purpose. I reassert, the power and supremacy of His Word remain intact, even though the context was changed.

While most of the blessings within this book had to be adapted into the form of a blessing, many of the blessings are literal quotations. For instance, the "Priestly (Aaronic) Blessing" from Numbers 6:24-26 is a blessing in its original context and is therefore quoted verbatim as one of the blessings in this book.

Format

To help the reader recognize modifications I made to form blessings, I used *italics* throughout the blessing chapters to highlight words I inserted for clarification or amplification. I did not use italics to emphasize the addition of words such as "may the Lord..." or "may you be blessed..." because this was done in nearly every verse to create the structure of a blessing.

I
The Positive & Negative Effect of Words

By the blessing of the upright a city is exalted, but by the mouth of the wicked it is torn down.
~ Proverbs 11:11 (NASB) ~

Words mean things. There are blessings and there are curses. Just as positive words breathe life, hope, and promise into the recipient, negative words breed death. Affirming words strengthen and encourage whereas negative words discourage and destroy.

Affirmation is essential for mental and emotional health. Personal experience tells us this is true. You may remember hugs from your father when he said, "I'm so proud of you." Perhaps you once saved a note from a grade school teacher that said, "Excellent work. I knew you could do it." These experiences made you feel good about yourself, boosted your confidence, and helped you see the possibilities for your future.

Similarly, who has not known the pain of negative words? "You're in my way!" or "What do you think you're doing?" Such comments may have left you feeling humiliated or embarrassed. Negative words tend to drain your enthusiasm and can cause you to doubt yourself.

Affirmation and a Whole Lot More

The Bible is not just a historical document. It is a *living* communication from God to us. The insights it provides are literally endless because they are revealed by the Holy Spirit as the Lord wills. Our spirits swell in affirmation each time we get a new glimpse into God's character, priorities, and unlimited resources. Our trust in God is strengthened as we allow ourselves to be saturated with His Word.

Let's review some important facets of His message that enable us to operate by faith and not by sight:

- God's plan for our salvation is compellingly spelled out through His recurring theme of forgiveness and redemption.

- He emphasizes the eternal nature of His being and of His covenant with Israel.

- He reveals the mystery of the Church, grafted into the tree of Israel to become joint heirs to the redemption and blessing reserved for His chosen ones.

- The Lord conveys His Fatherhood in the way He speaks about His love, mercy, compassion, grace, and favor toward us.

- God makes it clear that we have access to His power, authority, and protection through our divine inheritance.

- The Lord communicates our ability to exercise wisdom and knowledge, strength and courage because we have been inhabited by His Holy Spirit.

- He teaches us to speak words of life and to minister with His anointing.
- He convinces us we have the ability to think and behave differently by showing He has infused us with His character.
- God's Word demonstrates the value He places on marriage, family, and legacy.
- The Lord instructs us in how we are to bless Him, honor Him, and worship Him.
- God persuades us He is both willing and able to be our provider and our healer.
- He consoles us as our source of peace, rest, and joy.
- The Lord expresses His desire to abide with us and experience constant fellowship with us.

The Bible holds the keys to knowing God's will and direction for our lives. As we permit it, God's Word will guide us on our journey toward achieving the goals He established for us. If we are to follow His plan for our lives, it is essential that we also pattern the way we talk after the way God talks. The Bible says *"the speech of the righteous is a fountain of life..."* (Prov. 10:11a, CJB). May our words be a fountain of life. May our words be a fountain of blessing.

The "Anti-" Blessing

Proverbs 18:21 says, *"Death and life are in the power of the tongue"* (NASB). If the recitation of blessing speaks life, hope, affirmation, and promise then words that communicate death and despair need to be recognized as curses. Let me be clear, one does not have to practice occultism or witchcraft in order to pronounce a curse. This is a painful reality because many of us have spoken a curse into someone else's life, be it innocently or intentionally.

Whether or not we like to admit it, we can speak words that instill hopelessness and loss to others. Destructive phrases like, "You idiot," "Can't you do anything right?" or "You make me sick," cut like a knife and the impact can last for years...even a lifetime.

When our negative words resonate with the listener, they can reinforce vain imaginations and lies with which the person may already be struggling. It is terrible to think we could say something that would break someone's spirit or discourage them to the point of losing confidence in their ability to accomplish something worthwhile. We need to be aware that our misspoken words can influence another's self-image or contribute to a destructive change of direction in another person's life.

The more influence we have in someone's life, the more weight our words carry. I have more persuasion with my wife and my daughters than I do with an acquaintance or a group of strangers. Our words are powerful and so we must be on guard as to what we say and how we say it.

No Middle Ground

One of the most challenging truths we face is to recognize there is no such place as "middle ground" when it comes to the things of God. Jesus said, *"He that is not with me is against me"* (Luke 11:23, KJV). May we all keep this in mind as we choose our words. The things we say will either represent the principles of God's kingdom or of Satan's kingdom.

Jesus said, *"The mouth speaks what overflows from the heart"* (Matt. 12:34, CJB), and yet, *"The heart is deceitful above all things and desperately wicked"* (Jer. 17:9, KJV). Herein lies our challenge. It is impossible for us to speak what is *not* in our heart. Therefore we must cultivate and prune what grows in our heart.

If we apply this understanding, we should conclude that our words are rarely neutral, though we sometimes wish it to be the case. We need the Life of God to thrive in our hearts and govern our thoughts, actions, and words. The awareness that what we say can speak life or death must motivate us to carefully select our words. We have the opportunity and the responsibility to affirm and encourage others with the messages of God.

2
The Blessing

*Like apples of gold in settings of silver
is a word appropriately spoken.*
~ Proverbs 25:11 (CJB) ~

Throughout the history of mankind, words of blessing have been spoken over people, nations, land, livestock, weather conditions, and innumerable other objects and events. This ancient tradition is a powerful practice that produces supernatural consequences. The blessings of God Himself are recorded in numerous passages of Scripture. Jesus spoke blessings to the Father and to the people He encountered. We find many Biblical accounts of individuals – from patriarchs to apostles – imparting words of blessing.

Approximately 2500 years ago during the Babylonian exile, Ezra the Scribe and the Men of the Great Assembly established the content and order of the daily prayers. They are credited with deciding on the correct text for blessings that are recited in Jewish homes and synagogues to this day.[1]

Somewhere during the first two thousand years of the Church, this practice all but disappeared from the daily life of Christians. As a consequence, we have nearly abandoned the impartation of spoken blessings.

---

[1] Rabbi Abraham B. Witty and Rachel J. Witty, *Exploring Jewish Tradition* (New York: Doubleday, 2001), 50.

We often hear expressions such as, "God bless you" or "be blessed." Many choirs sing "The Lord bless thee and keep thee..." in churches on Sunday mornings. However, the purposeful speaking of blessing to dynamically touch the life of another with the power and authority of God seems all too rare.

As we study and restore this Biblical practice, we will come to discover the profound influence it can have on our families, our congregations, our society, and our own lives. This book provides a way to reintroduce this observance so that we can impact others with words of blessing, as priests of the Most High God.

What is a Blessing?

In the 21st century, the definition of "blessing" seems to vary, person by person. To some, a blessing is a prayer. For many, it is confined to the prayer said at meal times. Any warm thought or expression of good will might be considered a blessing. Many view a blessing as an impartation having sacramental-like attributes. For example, in Roman Catholicism, a person asks the priest to bless him before making a confession. To others, the blessing is a means of bringing God's influence into the life of another person. In reality, a blessing is all of these things.

We will define a blessing as "a spoken word that brings God's influence to a person or situation." God will faithfully influence people and situations if we prayerfully apply His Word under the guidance of His Holy Spirit. God wants to be actively involved in people's lives and He wants us to be part of the process, if we are willing to participate and remain in submission to His leadership.

To develop a complete understanding about blessings, we need to include a look at the Jewish perspective and practice. The life-style of blessing is deeply embedded in their culture and it dates back to the days of the Patriarchs. *Note*: please see Appendix A for a discussion of God's covenant with Israel and the Church.

The Hebrew word for blessing is "brachah." The word "brachah" appears sixty-nine times in the Old Testament and in sixty of those occurrences, it is translated "blessed," "blessing," "blessings," or "most blessed." Interestingly, this word comes from "berech," the root word meaning "knee," which reveals the association between blessing and bending one's knee in reverence. Kneeling is an acknowledgement of God's sovereignty and majesty.

To say a blessing is to "make a brachah." According to Jewish tradition, God's people hear His words in the Torah and God hears the words of His people when they recite a brachah.[2] The recitation of blessings is woven into the fabric of daily life for observant Jews because it maintains their awareness of total dependence upon God. This is revealed in the sentence structure of a brachah.

All brachot (plural) begin with the Hebrew word "baruch," meaning "blessed" or "praised" as part of the phrase, "Blessed are You, Lord our God, King of the Universe…" In other words, a brachah begins

---

[2] Rabbi Abraham B. Witty and Rachel J. Witty, *Exploring Jewish Tradition* (New York: Doubleday, 2001), 59.

by "recognizing God as the Source of all blessing." Therefore, recital of these blessings testifies to dependency upon God and proclaims readiness to accept His benevolence.

To this day, Orthodox Jews recite upwards of 100 blessings each and every day. A traditional brachah is available for nearly every aspect of life. There are blessings of praise and supplication, blessings for enjoyment of things that give pleasure, blessings of thanksgiving, and blessings associated with performing a commandment. The events for reciting a blessing range from consuming food or drink to smelling a fragrance to reading the Bible to recognizing that personal harm was averted.

We can learn from these Jewish faithful who have developed a consciousness that acknowledges the God of love as Creator of all things. They recognize Him as the sovereign King of the universe to whom they owe loving obedience. He is acknowledged as the Omniscient One who has a purpose and plan for all things. Perhaps the greatest virtue of the spoken blessing is that of transmitting the message of God's sovereignty. It is from His loving dominion that all blessings flow.

How to Bless – The Model Blessing

It should come as no surprise that God gave us a Model Blessing. Jesus gave us the Model Prayer, more commonly referred to the Lord's Prayer, recorded in two New Testament passages: Matthew 6:9-13 and Luke 11:1-4. Many of us have heard sermons and read books that unpacked "the model" for us. We understand Jesus' intent went far beyond adoption of His prayer as our one-and-only prayer. Rather, He gave us the Model Prayer as the representation of *how* we ought to pray.

We find the Model Blessing in chapter six of Numbers – the "Priestly Blessing" (also called the "Aaronic Blessing" or the "three-fold blessing"). *"Then the Lord spoke to Moses, saying, 'Speak to Aaron and to his sons, saying, "Thus you shall bless the sons of Israel. You shall say to them: the Lord bless you, and keep you; the Lord make His face shine on you, and be gracious to you; the Lord lift up His countenance on you, and give you peace." So they shall invoke My name on the sons of Israel, and I then will bless them'"* (Num. 6:22-27, NASB). As we dissect the Model Blessing, we will have a better understanding of the rich guidance it provides for *how* we are to bless.

"The Lord bless thee..." conveys God's impartation of *covenant benefits* to His children. In Deuteronomy 7:6-26 and 28:1-14, Moses enumerated some of the abundant blessings to be expected by those who obediently keep covenant with the Lord. In these passages (and others) God asserted He would provide rain in the right seasons, fertility among the people and their animals, healing of afflictions and diseases, overflowing provision, bountiful harvests, national prominence, and the defeat of their enemies. Just as God granted these extraordinary benefits to His covenant people, we are to bestow His blessings of life and health, provision and shelter to those who walk in covenant relationship with Him today.

"...And keep thee" expresses the *guardianship* of God. The Hebrew word *shamar* means to keep, guard, observe,

and give heed. When blessed with God's keeping, the Lord is rightly positioned as the divine source of protection against evil, sickness, poverty, and calamity. It is He alone who delivers our souls from death, keeps our eyes from tears, and our feet from stumbling.[3] Accordingly, God directs us to bless others with His custodial care and safekeeping.

"The Lord make his face to shine upon thee..." In this way, we are to pronounce blessings for God's *favor* and *friendship*. To cause the "face to shine upon" is a Biblical idiom for "to be friendly to him" or "to smile upon." We are also blessing for God's transforming *holiness* in the lives of those who accept His covenant. Throughout the Scriptures, "light" – ultimately emanating from the Lord – symbolizes holiness and purity. Therefore, recipients of His light become holy as He is holy. In addition, many rabbis interpret this phrase to speak of God's gift of knowledge, moral insight, or enlightenment.[4] Consequently, this expression also models the transference of God's *enlightenment* to those who seek Him.

"...And be gracious unto thee" communicates the *grace* God shows those who turn to Him as Lord. He does good things for those He loves, not because of entitlement, but because *He* is gracious and loving. This blessing implies that God graciously fulfills our petitions; He does not respond out of obligation. Some rabbinical commentators believe this blessing suggests

---

[3] Rabbi Dr. J.H. Hertz, *The Pentateuch and Haftorahs*, 2nd Edition (London: Soncino, 1960) 595
[4] Ibid.

God not only shows us His grace, but He gives us grace in the eyes of our fellow man.[5] In blessing this way, we therefore call upon the Lord to grant His unmerited favor toward us and to grant us His favor with other people.

"The Lord lift his countenance upon thee..." speaks of the *attentiveness* of God. The New International Version of the Bible says "the Lord turn his face toward you." The Hebrew word, *paniym*, meaning "face" or "countenance", is the same word used in the phrase above. However, the imagery here is one of a father responding to the tug of a little one at his feet..."Yes, my child?" As our heavenly Father, God delights in directing His loving care and attention toward us. He wants to be up close and personal with us. The Lord guides us to bless others with His accessibility and intimacy so they may enjoy the fellowship He wishes everyone to have with Him.

"...And give thee peace" declares God-given *peace* is available to covenant keepers. The Hebrew word for peace, *shalom*, is a powerful word connoting not only freedom *from* all disaster, but access *to* health, welfare, security, and tranquility. It is said that shalom is the peace that reconciles and strengthens. This peace calms and clears our vision, frees us from restlessness, and delivers us from the bondage of unsatisfied desire.[6] Jesus is quoted in John 14:27, *"Peace I leave with you, my peace I give unto you: not as the world giveth, give I unto you. Let not your heart be troubled, neither let it be afraid."*

---

[5] Ibid.
[6] Ibid.

Another translation of shalom is "completeness." It is interesting to keep this in mind as we read Colossians 2:10, "*And ye are complete in him (Jesus), which is the head of all principality and power.*" We could say the Model Blessing concludes with the ultimate attribute of all blessings. How fitting that God exhorts us to bless others with His gift of peace! For it is Jesus the Messiah, the Prince of Peace, in whom we find true peace…in whom we are made complete.

With this glimpse into the Model Blessing, we see the wide spectrum across which God directs us to bless. It is humbling to realize our heavenly Father extends the reach of His blessings *through us* as we are faithful to speak His blessings to others.

Why We Bless – Our Priestly Duty

There are a number of important reasons we speak blessings. First, our blessings convey that God is the loving, sovereign, omniscient Creator. God knows His role, but *we* often need to be reminded of it. When we recognize His eternal significance, it has a way of putting our earthly needs into perspective. He is great and we are small. "*The earth is the Lord's, and the fullness thereof; the world, and they that dwell therein*" (Ps. 24:1, KJV). "*He is before all things, and in Him all things hold together*" (Col. 1:17, NASB). We find great comfort when we embrace the Holy One who loved us enough to adopt us as His sons and daughters.

Second, our blessings invite God's involvement. As we speak blessings, we are prayerfully making declarations about God's promises and character. We are expressing our confidence in His intervention in our lives. We are petitioning the Lord to insert His power and authority into our situation, whether it is for healing, provision, favor, rescue, or direction. I have often heard news of tragic events and thought, "How can they possibly get through that without God?" In reality, *none of us* can get through *anything* without God! We must be diligent in asking God for His involvement in our lives and in the world around us.

Third, our blessings encourage and exhort the recipient. Something inside each of us, whether we are "lost" or "saved," recognizes Truth when it is spoken. To be informed or reminded that God's righteous, omnipotent hand is ready to touch us in our current condition gives us hope and encouragement.

Most importantly, our blessings release the blessing of God. We are acting as His ambassadors when we use His language to bless. Therefore, as we speak blessings to others, we are not merely sharing human thoughts. We are tangibly impacting their lives with divine authority.

The Bible gives us a mandate from God to speak blessings. In Numbers 6:22-27 we read, *"Then the Lord spoke to Moses, saying, 'Speak to Aaron and to his sons, saying, "Thus you shall bless the sons of Israel. You shall say to them: the Lord bless you, and keep you; the Lord make His face shine on you, and be gracious to you; the Lord lift up His countenance on you, and give you peace." So they shall invoke My name on the sons of Israel, and I then will bless them'"* (NASB).

When we read this passage, we tend to focus on the words of the "Priestly Blessing" itself but let's look at the sentences immediately preceding and following the blessing. We see that God commanded His priests to *speak the blessing of His Word* over the people *in order to bring His blessing upon them*! Only God can truly bless. The priests were selected to be instruments *through whom* God would bless. Let us look at this in practice.

Immediately after Aaron's first presentation of the offerings in his new role as High Priest, he raised his hands toward the people and blessed them. Soon thereafter, he and Moses together blessed the people. Leviticus 9:23 records that God then revealed His glory to all the people – fire came down from heaven and consumed the burnt offering on the altar.

The Lord was pleased with the obedience of Moses and Aaron in their consecration and commencement of the priesthood. He responded by blessing the people with the revelation of His glory and His acceptance of their offerings. In other words, Moses and Aaron invoked the name of the Lord on the people and God responded by blessing them. We find a reiteration of this teaching in Deuteronomy 21:5 and 1 Chronicles 23:13 where the priests were instructed to pronounce blessings over the people in the name of God.

Nearly 750 years later, King Hezekiah restored the temple, reinstituted all the functions of the priesthood, and convened a great Passover celebration in Jerusalem. As the feast concluded, *"The priests, who were Levites, stood up and blessed the people; Adonai heard their voice, and their prayer came up to the holy place where He lives, in heaven"* (2 Chron. 30:27, CJB). Again we find the priestly blessing noteworthy of facilitating access to God.

The exciting news is that we, as believers, are also priests of The Most High. The Apostle Peter told us, *"Ye are a chosen generation, a royal priesthood, an holy nation"* (1 Pet. 2:9a, KJV). The Apostle John wrote, *"Jesus Christ... has made us His Kingdom and His priests who serve before God His Father"* (Rev. 1:5-6, NLT). Serving as priests becomes part of our high calling when we accept Jesus as our Savior and Lord.

We have inherited some, not all, of the priestly duties from the Levitical priesthood dating back to the time of Moses. While some practices, such as offering sacrifices, are not applicable today, we are still expected to intercede on behalf of the people and to direct others in worship to God.[7] We also retain the important, though often overlooked, responsibility of imparting blessings upon God's people. Like other priestly duties, this is both a responsibility and a privilege. We can, and should, be speaking the blessing of God over others so that He will, in turn, bless them. Our blessings facilitate His direct blessings. It is our reasonable service to the Lord and it is our loving obligation to those around us.

Transformed by the Word

I believe another reason God commanded the priests to bring His blessing upon the people was to sanctify them. This world is corrupted by sin and sin leads to death. Despite that reality, the world's words and behaviors are competing to overtake and control our

---

[7] Dr. Sam Sasser and Dr. Judson Cornwall, *The Priesthood of the Believer* (New Brunswick: Bridge-Logos, 1999), 13.

hearts. We are constantly engaged in spiritual warfare yet victory results from the Lord's blessing.

We read about the lure of the world in Romans 12:2, *"Do not let yourselves be conformed to the standards of this world. Instead, keep letting yourselves be transformed by the renewing of your minds, so that you will know what God wants and will agree that what He wants is good, satisfying, and able to succeed"*(CJB). The "standards of this world" are self-focused. They promote thoughts and behaviors like hate, jealousy, lust, competitiveness, bigotry, condemnation, and so on. Consequently, words based on the world's standards are condemning, belittling, hurtful, and discouraging.

The Apostle Paul distilled this life-or-death matter down to a choice. We can either conform to the world and its standards or we can conform to God and His standards. The New Testament authors confronted nearly every conceivable sin. And each of those sins was at work within the Church. The ability, tendency, and temptation for those of us in the body of Christ to conform to the world's standards are beyond dispute. If we are honest with ourselves, we know this is true based on our own personal struggles, past or present.

In Matthew 12:34, Jesus said, *"For the mouth speaks what overflows from the heart."* The hearts of those in the world (that is, those who do not know Jesus as their Savior) are trapped in sin without God's Holy Spirit. Therefore curses come out of their mouths. When we allow their words to influence our minds and emotions (our "hearts") then we allow ourselves to conform to their standards.

In Romans 12:2, Paul gave us the key to transformation – our minds must be renewed by the Word. The more we saturate ourselves with the Word of God, the more we know what God wants, and the more we agree that what He wants is good, satisfying, and able to succeed.

Paul also wrote, *"Faith comes from hearing, and hearing by the word of Christ"* (Rom. 10:17, NASB). The Lord gives us faith to convert His Word into substantive beliefs. As we invest time in reading the Bible, our faith is built, our minds get renewed, and we are transformed from conformity to the world's standards into conformity to God's standards. Hallelujah!

Jesus taught us God's kingdom standards in Matthew 22:37-40, *"Jesus replied: 'Love the Lord your God with all your heart and with all your soul and with all your mind. This is the first and greatest commandment. And the second is like it: Love your neighbor as yourself. All the Law and the Prophets hang on these two commandments'"* (NIV). Here we discover that God's standards are selfless. They are based on preferring others to ourselves. We are to love God completely, with every fiber of our being, and we are to love others more than we love ourselves.

These are tall orders. They may seem reasonable as you read them right now. However, when you are having a "discussion" with your spouse, or you have been cut off in traffic, or the boss gives *your* promotion to a coworker, or a relationship is ended without explanation… that's when obeying these commandments can be challenging. In these moments, our ability to conform to the selfless standards of God's kingdom may appear beyond reach. Therefore, we must approach them with transformed perspectives from minds that have been renewed by the Word of God.

Heart Surgery

Remember Hebrews 4:12, *"The word of God is alive! It is at work and is sharper than any double-edged sword – it cuts right through to where soul meets spirit and joints meet marrow, and it is quick to judge the inner reflections and attitudes of the heart"* (CJB). I do not know where the soul meets the spirit, but I know what this verse says to me. It says only the living Word of God is able to help me distinguish between truth that is revealed by the Holy Spirit and the distorted thinking that comes through the filter of my emotions. I need the Living Word in me to transform my carnal thoughts and feelings into ideas and perspectives that align with God's truths.

As sinners, we constantly struggle to keep from conforming to the world's standards. We need to be overflowing with God's Word in order to transform our minds so that we can think and behave like Jesus. We need all the help we can get. Blessings are a means of imparting the Word to aid in this transformation. As we are blessed with God's Word, we increasingly operate with the character of The Master. In turn, we are able to function as the priests He intended us to be. Our priestly behavior is to include the speaking of blessings others.

3
Imparting Blessings

When and Whom to Bless

There is almost never a bad time for a blessing. Saying "goodbye" before heading out the door in the morning can be a time for blessing. Encouraging someone in their time of trouble can be an occasion for blessing. A hospital visit is definitely a moment for blessing. A note in a card for a birthday, graduation or any celebration is a perfect opportunity to speak blessing into someone else's life. As you begin to practice the priestly duty of blessing, you may be amazed by how frequently the Holy Spirit will nudge you to impart a blessing.

Parents may use this book to speak Scriptures in blessing their children and grandchildren. Spouses may speak blessings to strengthen their relationship with one another and affirm one another in ways they have never experienced. Siblings can bless siblings. Congregations can bless their pastors and pastors, their flocks. Friends may bless friends. Anyone who wants to impact the life of another person with the language of God can use blessings for that purpose.

Constructing a Blessing

A blessing can take different forms. Sometimes a blessing is a declaration, making a statement about who you are as a child of God or what you receive because you belong to Him.

> May you set the Lord continually before you;
> because He is at your right hand, you will not be shaken.
> Therefore may your heart be glad
> and may your glory rejoice;
> may your flesh also dwell securely.
> ~Psalm 16:8-9 (NASB) ~

Other times it is prayer-like, submitting a petition to the Lord.

> May God be a tower of salvation to you and may
> He show mercy to His anointed.
> ~ 2 Samuel 22:51 (NKJV) ~

Often a blessing is conditional upon the response and behavior of the one who receives the blessing, for example,

> May you seek first the kingdom of God
> and His righteousness and all the things you need
> shall be added unto you.
> ~ Matthew 6:33 (KJV) ~

A blessing may take on a prophetic tone.

> May the Spirit of the Lord fill you with power.
> May He help you do what is fair
> and may He make you brave.
> ~ Micah 3:8a (NIrV) ~

There are blessings having an instructional quality.

> May you know that you are a temple of God
> and that the Spirit of God dwells in you.
> ~ 1 Corinthians 3:16 (NASB) ~

In some blessings within this book, words and phrases are added to the Scripture text for clarity or amplification. Wherever this occurs, the additions are *italicized*.

> May the Lord train your hands for battle;
> may your arms *be able to* bend a bow of bronze.
> *Because God is the One who has called you,*
> *He will enable you to achieve results*
> *beyond any level you think to be possible.*
> ~ Psalm 18:34 (TNIV) ~

> May the Lord make a wide path for your feet
> to keep them from slipping. May you *allow God to*
> *stretch you out of your comfort zone and lead you*
> *into the destiny for which He designed you,*
> *confident He will not allow you to fail.*
> ~ 2 Samuel 22:37 & Psalm 18:36 (NLT) ~

> May the Lord prepare a table before you
> in the presence of your enemies,
> *even in the midst of oppression, tribulation, or fear.*
> ~ Psalm 23:5a (KJV) ~

I hope as your awareness of blessing grows through your use of this book, you will become sensitized to the many blessings contained in the Bible. My prayer is that you will begin to write and speak the blessings you glean from the Scriptures.

How to Use this Book

The blessings in this book are organized into categories and each category forms a chapter. This design makes it easy for you to find the blessings you feel are best suited for the person or situation at hand. For example, you might choose a blessing from among those dealing with *Wisdom, Knowledge, and Discernment* to speak over your child who is preparing for an important test. *Blessings for Peace, Rest & Patience* may be the right selection for your spouse who is anxious about an upcoming business presentation. *Blessings for Healing & Long Life* would be appropriate when visiting a sick friend in the hospital and *Blessings for Courage* may be the correct choice for a person who is fearful about air travel.

Every chapter begins with two supporting verses from the Bible and a brief explanation of how or why the blessings in the category apply. I encourage you to read each section introduction to help you become familiar with all the possibilities. Please understand there is nothing "sacred" about the way these blessings have been sorted. They are combined according to the way I have personally used them. It is up to you to use the blessings in whatever way you understand the Lord to be leading you.

You might choose to speak a blessing from the section I classified as *Blessings about Redemption & Restoration* because you feel it will bring encouragement to someone, not because the situation warrants a word about God's redemption or restoration. Please make these blessings *your* blessings by applying them in the manner *you* feel is most appropriate. In addition to familiarizing yourself with each chapter in the book, I urge you to always ask the Lord for guidance in selecting blessings He chooses for you to speak. As you are faithful to take this important step, I believe you will be delighted at the faithfulness and precision with which the Lord will lead you.

Over time, you will recognize that some blessings appear under more than one category. That is because they do have more than one application. Consider the blessing based on Psalm 18:35, *"May the Lord, who has given you the shield of His salvation, uphold you with His right hand; may His gentleness make you great"* (NASB). It appears under *Blessings about Redemption & Restoration* because it declares God's salvation. It is listed again under *Blessings about Destiny & Calling* because His gentleness makes you great. Your destiny with greatness is brought about through Him.

Two Unique Categories

I want to highlight two unique categories of blessing. *Blessings to God* are especially for those times when we bless the Lord...a "brachah." Just like Noah, King David, and the Apostle Paul, we want to be faithful in blessing the Lord. I hope you will make these blessings a part of your everyday life.

Blessings over Israel allow us to obey God and receive a blessing for ourselves at the same time. *"I will bless those who bless you, and the one who curses you I will curse, and in you, all the families of the earth will be blessed"* (Gen. 12:3, CJB) is a theme from the heart of God that permeates the Scriptures. Let us all be faithful to bless Israel as a regular part of our prayer lives. It will surely please our heavenly Father. *"For Zion's sake I will not keep silent, and for Jerusalem's sake I will not keep quiet, until her righteousness goes forth like brightness, and her salvation like a torch that is burning"* (Isa. 62:1, NKJV).

Laying on of Hands

When possible, I like to lay one, or both, hands on the head, shoulder, or back of a person as I bless them. This "laying on of hands" follows an example we find throughout Scripture. In Genesis chapter 27, Jacob disguised himself to "feel" like his brother when Isaac touched him and thereby received Esau's blessing. When Israel (Jacob) blessed Joseph's sons (Genesis 48), he crossed his hands so that he could bless Ephraim, the younger one, with his right hand, and he placed his left hand on Manasseh, even though he was the firstborn. Moses laid his hands on Joshua when he commissioned him before Eleazar the high priest and before the entire congregation, just as the Lord had instructed him (Num. 27:23).

In Matthew 19:13 (and Mark 10:16), we see that Jesus laid His hands upon the children as He blessed them. Jesus also laid His hands on the sick and healed them (Mark 6:5 & 8:23-25, Luke 4:40 & 13:13). The "chosen seven" (Deacons) who were selected to assist the apostles were ordained with the laying on of hands (Acts 6:6). In Acts 8:17, Peter and John laid their hands on the new Samaritan believers that they might receive the Holy Spirit. The Lord directed Ananias to lay hands on Saul, blinded from his encounter with Jesus on the road to Damascus, so that he might regain his sight (Acts 9:12). Paul and Barnabas were dedicated for their first missionary journey with the laying on of hands (Acts 13:3). And in 2 Timothy 1:6, Paul reminded Timothy to *"kindle afresh the gift of God which is in you through the laying on of my hands"* (NASB).

Whenever possible, the impartation of blessing accompanied by the laying on of hands permits us to follow a Biblical pattern established by the Patriarchs, the Apostles, and the Master Himself.

Go and Do Thou Likewise

Now it is time to put into practice all that we have been discussing. Familiarize yourself with the categories and the blessings in the pages that follow. Soon you will be speaking life-giving words to others. A good place to start is with those who are closest to you. Ask the Lord to show you what blessings He would like you to share on His behalf.

Please feel free to adapt these blessings as you speak them. I often like to personalize a blessing by inserting the name of the person to whom I am speaking. Sometimes I omit or add words spontaneously as I read a blessing. The important thing is to be led by the Spirit. Trust that you hear Him as He guides you.

Remember, as a priest of the Most High God, you are speaking the blessing of His Word over people in order to bring His blessing upon them. As an ambassador of the King of Kings, you are speaking the King's language to communicate on His behalf. We can never be more confident of our alignment with God than when we are speaking His own Word.

May you develop a life-style of blessing as you impact others' lives with the language of God!

May the Lord instruct you and teach you
in the way you are to go.
*Be confident because He will give you counsel
and His eyes will be watching you.*
~ Psalm 32:8 (CJB) ~

May you be confident of this very thing,
that He who has begun a good work in you
will complete it until the day of Jesus Christ.
~ Philippians 1:6 (NKJV) ~

4
Blessings about Redemption & Restoration

Salvation belongs to the Lord.
~ Psalm 3:8 (NASB) ~

*For God so loved the world,
that He gave His only begotten Son,
that whosoever believeth in Him
should not perish, but have everlasting life.*
~ John 3:16 (KJV) ~

Because God's truth sets people free, it is essential that we speak His words of life to those who need to receive His salvation. God's Word reveals the simplicity with which we can accept His forgiveness for sin through the atonement of Christ's sacrifice on the cross. The Bible describes how our faith in Jesus' supreme act of redemption allows us to become children of God and entitles us to spend eternity with Him in heaven.

The journey to restoration may require forgiving ourselves or forgiving others. The truth of Scripture is vital in helping us, as believers, recognize our legal right to walk away from our old natures and be transformed by the renewing of our minds. Discovering all the facets of redemption or restoration can be a process. God's Word will guide us through the steps to wholeness in Him.

May God give you new life and take care of you in your old age (Ruth 4:15a, NCV).

May the Lord raise you from the dust and may He lift you from the ash heap; may He seat you with princes and may you inherit a throne of honor (1 Sam. 2:8, NIV).

May you be *consciously aware that* God has given you the shield of His salvation; His help makes you great (2 Sam. 22:36, NASB).

The Lord your God is gracious and merciful, and will not turn away His face from you, if you return unto him (2 Chron. 30:9b, KJV).

May the good Lord provide atonement for everyone who prepares his heart to seek God, the Lord God of his fathers (2 Chron. 30:18-19, NKJV).

When you return and cry out to the Lord, may He hear you from heaven and may He deliver you many times according to His mercies (Neh. 9:28, NKJV).

May you have trust in God's mercy; and may your heart rejoice in your salvation (Ps. 13:5, KJV).

May the Lord, who has given you the shield of His salvation, uphold you with His right hand; may His gentleness make you great (Ps. 18:35, NASB).

May God look upon your affliction and your trouble, and may He forgive all your sins (Ps. 25:18, NASB).

May the Lord redeem you and show you favor (Ps. 26:11b, CJB).

Blessed is he whose transgression is forgiven, whose sin is covered (Ps. 32:1, KJV).

Happy is the person whom the Lord does not consider guilty and in whom there is nothing false (Ps. 32:2, NCV).

May the Lord forgive all your iniquities and may He heal all your diseases (Ps. 103:3, NKJV).

May God redeem your life from the pit and may He crown you with lovingkindness and compassion (Ps. 103:4, NASB).

May the Lord, who is righteous, cut you free from the cords of the wicked (Ps. 129:4b, NIV).

May you be confident you will never be uprooted *from your secure place with God, because Jesus' saving grace has made you* righteous (Prov. 10:30a, TNIV).

Behold, God is your salvation, may you trust *in Him* and not be afraid; for the Lord God is your strength and song, and He has become your salvation. Therefore may you joyously draw water from the springs of salvation (Isa. 12:2-3, NASB).

May you *know and embrace this:* if you come back to God and trust in Him, you will be saved (Isa. 30:15b, NCV).

May you delight greatly in the Lord; may your soul rejoice in your God. For He has clothed you with garments of salvation and arrayed you in a robe of righteousness, as a bridegroom adorns his head like a priest, and as a bride adorns herself with her jewels (Isa. 61:10, NIV).

May you return to your God, may you observe kindness and justice, and may you wait for your God continually (Hosea 12:6, NASB).

May you *tear* your heart and not your garments. Return to the Lord your God, for He is gracious and compassionate, slow to anger and abounding in love, and He relents from sending calamity. God will repay you for the years the locusts have eaten (*any unfortunate circumstances you faced or consequences you reaped because of your past choices*). You will have plenty to eat, until you are full, and you will praise the name of the Lord your God, who has worked wonders for you (Joel 2:13, 25-26, NIV).

May you know that salvation comes from the Lord alone (Jonah 2:9b, NLT).

For you who fear *the* name *of the Lord*, the Sun of Righteousness will rise with healing in His wings and you will go free, leaping with joy like calves let out to pasture (Mal. 4:2, NLT).

May you *know that you are free to walk without* any condemnation because you are in Christ Jesus. May you not walk according to the flesh, but according to the Spirit. For the law of the Spirit of life in Christ Jesus has made you free from the law of sin and death. *May you be encouraged to walk in the freedom of holiness and may you have the strength to resist temptation* (Rom. 8:1-2, NKJV).

May the source of your life be Christ Jesus, whom God has made our wisdom, our righteousness, our sanctification and our redemption (1 Cor. 1:30, RSV).

May you be blessed with grace and peace from God the Father and from our Lord Jesus Christ, who gave Himself for our sins, that He might deliver us from this present evil world, according to the will of God our Father (Gal. 1:3-4, KJV).

May you know the will of God, in keeping with the promise of life that is in Christ Jesus (2 Tim. 1:1, TNIV).

May the blood of Christ, who through the eternal Spirit offered Himself without spot to God, purge your conscience from dead works *so that you can* serve the living God (Heb. 9:14, KJV).

May you praise God, the Father of our Lord Jesus Christ! In His great mercy He has given you new birth into a living hope through the resurrection of Jesus Christ from the dead, and into an inheritance that can never perish, spoil or fade – kept in heaven for you (1 Pet. 1:3-4, NIV).

May you be strong, may the Word of God live in you, and may you overcome the evil one (1 John 2:14b, NIV).

May you keep yourself in the love of God, looking for the mercy of our Lord Jesus Christ unto eternal life (Jude 1:21, NKJV).

5
Blessings for God's Abiding Presence

*"But this is the covenant which I will make with the
house of Israel after those days," declares the Lord,
"I will put My law within them and on their heart I will
write it; and I will be their God,
and they shall be My people."*
~ Jeremiah 31:33 (NASB) ~

*And I will pray the Father,
and He shall give you another Comforter,
that He may abide with you forever.*
~ John 14:16 (KJV) ~

As children of God, we long to be in His presence. Sometimes we need reassurance that His Spirit actually dwells within us. There is a unique security that comes when we sense the touch of our Father's hand. At times, we want to crawl up into His lap. In other moments, we want to know His greatness is towering over our situation as He casts His shadow upon us.

The Lord anticipated our need for ongoing contact with Him and so He recorded His Word for us and gave us His Spirit. He is our constant companion because He lives in us. He goes before us and He stands over us. We find safekeeping in God's presence.

May God look on *you and have* concern for you (Exod. 2:25, NIV).

May *the Lord* pay close attention to you (Exod. 3:16, CJB).

May *the Lord* come to you and bless you wherever He causes His name to be honored (Exod. 20:24, NIV).

May the presence of *the Lord* be with you wherever you go. *In this way, may people* know you have found favor in the sight of *the Lord*. The presence of God is what distinguishes you from all the people *in the world who do not know Him* (Exod. 33:15-16, CJB).

May the Lord bless you and keep you; may the Lord make His face shine upon you, and be gracious to you; may the Lord lift up His countenance upon you, and give you peace (Num. 6:24-26, NKJV).

May the eyes of the Lord your God always be upon you, from the beginning of the year to the end of the year (Deut. 11:12, CJB).

May you eat your offerings in the presence of the Lord. May you rejoice over everything you set out to do in which the Lord your God has blessed you, you and your household (Deut. 12:7, CJB).

May God be a tower of salvation to you and may He show mercy to *you*...His anointed *one* (2 Sam. 22:51, NKJV).

May the Lord our God be with you as He was *when He led the children of Israel into the Promised Land*: may He not leave you or forsake you (1 Kings 8:57, KJV).

May the Lord be with you and may you prosper (1 Chron. 22:11b, NKJV).

May you enter the house of the Lord because of His great grace and love (Ps. 5:7, CJB).

May the Lord show you the path of life. In His presence is fullness of joy and at His right hand are pleasures forevermore (Ps. 16:11, NKJV).

May you dwell in the house of the Lord all the days of your life, to behold the beauty of the Lord, and to enquire in His temple (Ps. 27:4a, KJV).

Blessed are those who live in the Lord's house. They are always praising Him (Ps. 84:4, NIrV).

May you dwell in the secret place of the most High and *may you* abide under the shadow of the Almighty (Ps. 91:1, KJV).

May the Lord cover you with His feathers, and under His wings may you find refuge; His faithfulness will be your shield and rampart (Ps. 91:4, NIV).

May the Lord remember you and bless you (Ps. 115:12a, NIV).

May you walk before the Lord in the land of the living (Ps. 116:9, KJV).

May the Lord be near to you when you call on Him; He is close to all who call on Him in truth (Ps. 145:18, NIV).

May the Lord put His words in your mouth and may He cover you with the shadow of His hand (Isa. 51:16a, NKJV).

The Book of Blessings: Impacting Lives with the Language of God

May the Spirit of the Lord God be upon you (Isa. 61:1, KJV).

May you diligently seek to know the Lord and may you know that He will come as certain as the morning. May He come to you like rain, like the spring rains that water the earth (Hosea 6:3, CJB).

May the Lord your God, as a victorious warrior, *be* in your midst...*at all times...no matter where you may be*. He will *rejoice* over you with joy, He will be quiet in His love *for you*, He will rejoice over you with shouts of joy (Zeph. 3:17, NASB).

May the Spirit *of God* abide *with you* (in your midst) and may you not be afraid (Hag. 2:5b, NASB).

May you know that you are a temple of God and that the Spirit of God dwells in you (1 Cor. 3:16, NASB).

May you *see*, with open face beholding as in a glass, the glory of the Lord, and may you be changed into *His* image from glory to glory, even as by the Spirit of the Lord (2 Cor. 3:18, KJV).

May God, out of His glorious riches, strengthen you with power through His Spirit in your inner being, so that Christ may dwell in your heart through faith (Eph. 3:16-17a, NIV).

May you, being rooted and established in love, have power, together with all the saints, to grasp how wide and long and high and deep is the love of Christ, and to know this love that surpasses knowledge – and may you be filled to the measure of all the fullness of God (Eph. 3:17b-19, NIV).

Speaking the truth in love, may *you* grow up into Him in all things, which is the head, even Christ (Eph. 4:15, KJV).

May you draw near with confidence to the throne of grace, so that you may receive mercy and find grace to help in time of need (Heb. 4:16, NASB).

May you be built up in your most holy faith as you pray in union with the Holy Spirit (Jude 1:20, CJB).

6
Blessings about God's Word

*Thy word is a lamp unto my feet,
and a light unto my path.*
~ Psalm 119:105 (KJV) ~

*As for God, His way is perfect;
The word of the Lord is proven.*
~ Psalm 18:30a (NKJV) ~

King David, the Psalmist, loved the Word of God. Job said, "*I have esteemed the words of His mouth, more than my necessary food*" (Job 23:12, KJV). The book of Hebrews revealed, "*The Word of God is alive and powerful…*"

Our faith is built up by the Word of God. Through the Scriptures, we learn what the Lord wants us to know about His character and behavior. The more we read it, the better we know Him. The Bible explains God's expectations for us and it reveals His eternal plans. It is our guidebook for life and it contains an inventory of God's abundant provisions. Let us bless others to embrace the Word of God and
its life-changing potential.

May you be strong and very courageous; may you be careful to do according to all the law of Moses. *May you be faithful to God's Word and* not turn from it to the right or to the left, so that you may have success wherever you go (Josh. 1:7, NASB).

May you be blessed as you are faithful not to let the Book of the Law depart from your mouth. *May you be faithful to* meditate on it day and night so that you will be careful to do everything written in it. Then you will be prosperous and successful (Josh. 1:8, NIV).

May you know that God's way is perfect; may you know the Word of the Lord is flawless (2 Sam. 22:31a, NIV).

May you not depart from the command of God's lips; may you treasure the words of His mouth more than your necessary food (Job 23:12b, NASB).

May you love the Lord's teachings, and may you think about those teachings day and night. As you do, you will be strong, like a tree planted by a river. The tree produces fruit in season, and its leaves don't die. Everything you do will succeed (Ps. 1:2-3, NCV).

Blessed are those who keep *the* testimonies *of God*, who seek Him with *their* whole heart! They also do no iniquity; they walk in His ways (Ps. 119:2-3, NKJV).

May the Lord open your eyes to see the miracles in His teachings (Ps. 119:18, NCV).

May you be continually consumed with longing for God's rulings (Ps. 119:20, CJB).

May the covenant laws of the Lord be your delight. May they give you wise advice (Ps. 119:24, NIrV).

May God make you understand the way of His precepts and may you meditate on His wonders (Ps. 119:27, NASB).

May the decrees of God be the theme of your song wherever you lodge (Ps. 119:54, NIV).

May the Word of the Lord be a lamp for your feet and a light on your path (Ps. 119:105, NLT).

May the Lord's testimonies be your heritage forever and may they be the rejoicing of your heart (Ps. 119:111, KJV).

May the Lord be your hiding place and your shield. May you put your hope in His Word (Ps. 119:114, NKJV).

May the unfolding of God's words give light and understanding to you (Ps. 119:130, NASB).

May you be happy because you obey what you have been taught from the Word of God (Prov. 29:18b, NCV).

May you *continually receive and trust* the Word of God. Every word is pure. May the Lord be a shield to you as you put your trust in Him (Prov. 30:5, NKJV).

May you hear the words of God and act on them *so that you will be* like a wise man who built his house on rock (Matt. 7:24, NASB).

May you *always be* a rich, *fertile soil, ready to receive the life containing seed that is the Word of God*. May His Word sprout in you, grow, and yield a bountiful harvest...30, 60, and even 100 times what He has sown and will sow in you (Mark 4:8, CJB).

May you be blessed with ears that listen *and may you understand the Word of the Lord* (Mark 4:9, NIrV).

May you powerfully refute *all skepticism and resistance raised against God,* demonstrating by the Scriptures that Jesus *is* the Christ (Acts 18:28, NASB).

May you be a blameless and innocent *child* of God, without blemish in the midst of a crooked and perverse generation, among whom you *will* shine as *a* light in the world, *as you* hold fast the Word of Life (Phil. 2:15-16a, RSV).

May the Word of Christ dwell in you richly in all wisdom *as you* teach and admonish *others* in psalms and hymns and spiritual songs, singing with grace in your heart to the Lord (Col. 3:16, KJV).

May you be like a newborn baby, desiring the pure milk of the Word that you may grow thereby (1 Pet. 2:2, NKJV).

May you be strong, may the Word of God live in you, and may you overcome the evil one (1 John 2:14b, NIV).

7
Blessings for God's Favor

A good man obtains favor from the Lord.
~ Proverbs 12:2a (NKJV) ~

And the king granted him all he requested
because the hand of the Lord his God was upon him.
~ Ezra 7:6b (NASB) ~

It doesn't take long in our journey with the Lord to realize we are nothing without Him. Any value we possess has been placed in us by Him. We have no intrinsic goodness, apart from God. Each and every gift and talent has been given to us by our heavenly Father...without exception.
We desperately need the favor of God and the rich deposits with which He equips us to fulfill our destinies. We will effectively engage life when the Lord's hand is upon us and *only* when the Lord's hand is upon us. Let us be faithful to enhance the lives we touch by
asking God's hand of favor
to rest upon them.

May God look on *you and have* concern for you (Exod. 2:25, NIV).

May the Lord pay close attention to you (Exod. 3:16, CJB).

May the presence of *the Lord* be with you wherever you go. *In this way, may people* know you have found favor in the sight of *the Lord*. The presence of God is what distinguishes you from all the people *in the world who do not know Him* (Exod. 33:15-16, CJB).

May you find favor in the sight of the Lord and may He know you by name (Exod. 33:17, CJB).

May the Lord bless you and keep you; may the Lord make His face shine upon you, and be gracious to you; may the Lord lift up His countenance upon you, and give you peace (Num. 6:24-26, NKJV).

May the Lord protect you, care for you, and guard you like the pupil of His eye, as an eagle that stirs up her nest, hovers over her young, spreads out her wings, takes them, and carries them as she flies (Deut. 32:10b-11, CJB).

May the Lord make you strong and be pleased with the work you do (Deut. 33:11, NCV).

May you be satisfied with favor and full of the blessing of the Lord (Deut. 33:23a, NKJV).

May you be blessed *by* the Lord who has not withdrawn His kindness *from* the living *or from* the dead (Ruth 2:20b, NASB).

May you gain favor with the Lord and with all people (1 Sam. 2:26, NLT).

May your life be valued much in the eyes of the Lord and may He deliver you out of all tribulation (1 Sam. 26:24, NKJV).

May you be *consciously aware that* God has given you the shield of His salvation; His help makes you great (2 Sam. 22:36, NASB).

May God bless you and enlarge your territory! May the hand of God be with you and keep you from harm so that you will be free from pain (1 Chron. 4:10b, NIV).

May the hand of the Lord be upon you (1 Kings 18:46, KJV).

May the Word of the Lord be with you (2 Kings 3:12, KJV).

May the hand of the Lord come upon you (2 Kings 3:15, KJV).

May the hand of God give you one heart *with others in His kingdom* to do *what your leaders have directed* by the Word of the Lord (2 Chron. 30:12, KJV).

May *your commitment* to walk in covenant relationship with the Lord and wholeheartedly obey His Word *encourage others to stand with you in* affirming their covenant with God (2 Chron. 34:31-32, CJB).

May you be strengthened according to the hand of the Lord your God upon you (Ezra 7:28b, NASB).

May *the Lord make you like Esther, may you* find favor and kindness with the King *of Kings* (Esther 2:17, NASB).

May God weigh you in honest scales and find you blameless, having been made the righteousness of God in Christ Jesus (Job 31:6, 2 Cor. 5:21 NIV).

The Lord blesses the godly, surrounding them with His shield of love (Ps. 5:12, NLT).

May you *know with confidence* that you will never be moved from your place of rest in the tent of the Lord or from life on His holy mountain (Ps. 15:1, CJB).

May God remember all your gifts and may He look favorably on your offerings (Ps. 20:3, NLT).

May the Lord grant you your heart's desire and bring all your plans to success (Ps. 20:4, CJB).

May the Lord give you all that you ask for (Ps. 20:5b, NCV).

May goodness and mercy surely follow you all the days of your life, and may you dwell in the house of the Lord forever (Ps. 23:6, KJV).

The Lord shares His plans with you *because you* have respect for Him. He will make His covenant known to you (Ps. 25:14, NIrV).

May the Lord turn to you and show you favor (Ps. 25:16, CJB).

May you feast on the abundance of God's house; may He give you drink from His river of delights (Ps. 36:8, NIV).

May God give you victory. You will succeed because of the Lord's mighty power; you will succeed because He favors you and smiles on you (Ps. 44:3, NLT).

May the Lord show you *His* favor and *may you know you can* go to Him for safety (Ps. 57:1a, NIrV).

May God look with favor on you; you have been appointed by Him (Ps. 84:9, NIrV).

May the Lord God be your sun and shield; may the Lord give you grace and glory; no good thing does He withhold from those who walk uprightly (Ps. 84:11, NASB).

May the Lord give you a sign of His favor so that others will see it. As they see His sign of favor upon you, may all people know the Lord has helped you and comforted you (Ps. 86:17, CJB).

May the Lord our God treat you well. May He give you success in what you do; yes, give you success in what you do (Ps. 90:17, NCV).

May the Lord answer you when you call upon Him and may He be with you when you are in trouble. May He deliver you and bring you honor (Ps. 91:15, NIV).

May the Lord remember you and bless you (Ps. 115:12a, NIV).

May you be blessed by the Lord, who made heaven and earth (Ps. 115:15, NCV).

May the Lord be near to you when you call on Him; He is close to all who call on Him in truth (Ps. 145:18, NIV).

May you win favor and esteem in the sight of God and of people (Prov. 3:4, CJB).

May you find wisdom *and, in doing so,* find life and win approval from the Lord (Prov. 8:35, NLT).

May you *know the Lord sees you, His bride,* like the sunrise in all of its glory. You are to Him as beautiful as the moon, as bright as the sun, as majestic as troops carrying their banners (Song of Sol. 6:10, NIrV).

May *Jesus the Bridegroom* set you as a seal upon His heart, as a seal upon His arm (Song of Sol. 8:6a, NKJV).

May God engrave you on the palms of His hands (Isa. 49:16, CJB).

May the Lord hear you when you call to Him and answer you. May He show you great and mighty things, which you do not know (Jer. 33:3, NKJV).

May God have compassion for you according to the multitude of His mercies (Lam. 3:32b, KJV).

May the Lord plant you *in the midst of that which He has promised you*; may you no more be pulled up out of the *promises* He has given you (Amos 9:15, KJV).

May you increase in wisdom and stature, and in favor with God and man (Luke 2:52, KJV).

I commit you to the love and kindness of the Lord (Acts 15:40, CJB).

May you *keep* growing in the special favor and knowledge of our Lord and Savior Jesus Christ (2 Pet. 3:18, NLT).

8
Blessings for God's Guidance

Trust in the Lord with all thine heart;
and lean not unto thine own understanding.
In all thy ways acknowledge Him,
and He shall direct thy paths.
~ Proverbs 3:5-6 (KJV) ~

Guide me in Your truth and teach me,
for You are the God who saves me,
my hope is in You all day long.
~ Psalm 25:5 (CJB) ~

The voyage isn't worth making unless God is at the wheel. We have all headed down blind alleys because we took a turn without consulting Him. *"There is a way that seemeth right unto a man, but the end thereof are the ways of death"* (Prov. 16:25, KJV). We need the guidance of our omniscient Father. He is the source of wisdom, He transcends time and place, and He loves us more than we love ourselves. His Word clearly expresses His desire to teach and lead us.

May *God* help you speak and teach you what to do (Exod. 4:15, NIV).

May *the* Lord *be your* Banner, *Jehovah Nissi* (Exod. 17:15, NIV).

May *the Lord* send an angel ahead of you to guard you along *your* way and *may He* bring you to the place He has prepared *for you* (Exod. 23:20, NIV).

May *the Lord* fill *you* with the Spirit of God – with skill, ability and knowledge *concerning everything He has called you to do* (Exod. 31:3, NIV).

May the Lord endow you with the wisdom to carry out every assignment He has given you (Exod. 31:6, CJB).

May the Lord be your lamp and may the Lord lighten your darkness (2 Sam. 22:29, KJV).

May the Lord make a wide path for your feet to keep them from slipping. *May you allow God to stretch you out of your comfort zone. Be confident He will not allow you to fail* (2 Sam. 22:37 & Ps. 18:36, NLT).

May you serve God with a whole heart and a willing mind; for the Lord searches all hearts and understands every intent of the thoughts. If you seek Him, He will let you find Him (1 Chron. 28:9, NASB).

May the Lord, the God of our ancestors, the God of Abraham, Isaac, and Jacob, make us want to serve Him always, and make us want to obey Him (1 Chron. 29:18, NCV).

May the Lord be with you when you are with Him. And if you seek Him, He will let you find Him (2 Chron. 15:2b, NASB).

May you understand the visions of God, and as long as you seek the Lord, may He make you to prosper (2 Chron. 26:5, KJV).

May the Lord show you the path of life. In His presence is fullness of joy and at His right hand are pleasures forevermore (Ps. 16:11, NKJV).

May the Lord light your candle; may the Lord your God enlighten your darkness (Ps. 18:28, KJV).

May the Lord restore your soul, may He lead you in the paths of righteousness for His name's sake (Ps. 23:3, KJV).

May the Lord make His ways known to you and may He teach you His paths (Ps. 25:4, NASB).

May God lead you in His truth and teach you, for He is the God of your salvation; may you wait on Him all the day (Ps. 25:5, NKJV).

May you *have a healthy fear of the Lord and receive the blessing of all those who fear Him.* May the Lord instruct you in the way *He has* chosen for you (Ps. 25:12, NIV).

May the Lord make you wise and show you where *He wants you* to go. May He guide you and watch over you (Ps. 32:8, NCV).

Blessed is the man whom the Lord corrects. Blessed is the person God teaches from His law. He gives him rest from times of trouble (Ps. 94:12-13a, NIrV).

May you trust in the Lord with all your heart and lean not on your own understanding; in all your ways submit to Him, and He will make your paths straight (Prov. 3:5-6, TNIV).

May the Lord direct you in the way of wisdom; may He lead you in upright paths. *As you allow Him to guide your* walk, your steps will not be impeded; and if you run, you will not stumble (Prov. 4:11-12, NASB).

May your path be like the first gleam of dawn, shining ever brighter till the full light of day (Prov. 4:18, NIV).

May the way of the Lord be strength to you. You are His upright one(s) (Prov. 10:29, KJV).

The path of life is level for those who are right with God; may the Lord make the way of life smooth for you (Isa. 26:7, NCV).

The Lord knows the plans He has for you, plans for welfare and not for calamity to give you a future and a hope. *May you embrace this truth* – when you call upon the Lord and pray to Him, He will listen to you. You will seek the Lord and find Him when you search for Him with all your heart (Jer. 29:11-13, NASB).

9
Blessings for God's Mercy, Grace, & Compassion

*The steadfast love of the Lord never ceases,
His mercies never come to an end;
they are new every morning;
great is Thy faithfulness.*
~ Lamentations 3:22-23 (RSV) ~

*Let us therefore come boldly unto the throne of grace,
that we may obtain mercy,
and find grace to help in time of need.*
~ Hebrews 4:16 (KJV) ~

Because we are human, we are inherently imperfect. We sometimes find ourselves entangled in situations we have created due to our own sin, error, or lack of discernment.

Other life scenarios may simply be the consequence of living in a sin-tainted world – the loss of a job, a divorce, the death of a loved one, or a chronic illness in a child. In all these circumstances and more, we need the mercy and grace of the Lord. At times, our very survival may require it.

Our human capacity for self-pity and feelings of hopelessness can be obliterated by the compassion of the Lord. However, we must allow Him to minister to our needs as He desires. If we invite Him, His lovingkindness will engulf us.

May Adonai your God keep with you the covenant and mercy He swore to the children of Israel (Deut. 7:12, CJB).

May God be a tower of salvation to you and may He show mercy to *you*…His anointed one (2 Sam. 22:51, NKJV).

When you cry out to the Lord, may He hear you from heaven and may He deliver you many times according to His mercies (Neh. 9:28, NKJV).

May God remember you and spare you according to the greatness of His mercy (Neh. 13:22b, KJV).

May you enter the house of the Lord because of His great grace and love (Ps. 5:7, CJB).

May you have trust in God's mercy and may your heart rejoice in your salvation (Ps. 13:5, KJV).

May goodness and mercy surely follow you all the days of your life, and may you dwell in the house of the Lord forever (Ps. 23:6, KJV).

May you *rejoice in the Lord*, for He hears your cry for mercy (Ps. 28:6, TNIV).

May the Lord show you His amazing grace (Ps. 31:21a, CJB).

May the Lord's unfailing love rest upon you, even as you put your hope in Him (Ps. 33:22, NIV).

May the Lord be gracious to you as you wait for Him. May He be your arm every morning, your salvation also in the time of trouble (Isa. 33:2, NKJV).

Blessings for God's Mercy, Grace, & Compassion

May you be blessed with the love and kindness of the Lord (Acts 15:40, CJB).

May you be blessed with grace and peace from God our Father, and the Lord Jesus Christ (Rom. 1:7b, KJV).

May grace be unto you, and peace, from God our Father, and from the Lord Jesus Christ (1 Cor. 1:3, KJV).

May you *walk in* the grace God has given you in Christ Jesus. May you be made rich in every way, in all your speaking and in all your knowledge (1 Cor. 1:4-5, NCV).

May you be blessed with grace and peace from God the Father and from our Lord Jesus Christ, who gave Himself for our sins, that He might deliver us from this present evil world, according to the will of God our Father (Gal. 1:3-4, KJV).

May you be given grace according to the measure of Christ's gift, *in other words...endless grace* (Eph. 4:7, NKJV).

May the grace of the Lord Jesus Christ be with you (Phil. 4:23, NCV).

May grace, mercy, and peace *be yours* from God the Father and Christ Jesus our Lord (1 Tim. 1:2b, NCV).

May the grace of the Lord pour out on you abundantly, along with the faith and love that are in Christ Jesus (1 Tim. 1:14, NIV).

May you draw near with confidence to the throne of grace, so that you may receive mercy and find grace to help in time of need (Heb. 4:16, NASB).

May you praise God, the Father of our Lord Jesus Christ! In His great mercy He has given you new birth into a living hope through the resurrection of Jesus Christ from the dead, and into an inheritance that can never perish, spoil or fade – kept in heaven for you (1 Pet. 1:3-4, NIV).

May grace and peace be multiplied unto you through the knowledge of God, and of Jesus our Lord (2 Pet. 1:2, KJV).

May you keep yourself in the love of God, looking for the mercy of our Lord Jesus Christ unto eternal life (Jude 1:21, NKJV).

10
Blessings for God's Protection & Safety

God is my strength and protection;
He makes my way go straight.
~ 2 Samuel 22:33 (NASB) ~

God is our refuge and strength,
a very present help in trouble.
~ Psalm 46:1 (KJV) ~

Fear, trials, and tribulation have a way of eliciting prayer. People who otherwise profess no faith in God will often turn to Him in life-threatening situations. As believers, we know-that-we-know our help comes from the Lord…continually.

We know security systems don't really protect us from intruders and armies don't truly defend us from invaders. Vitamins, exercise and nutrition aren't our ultimate defenses against sickness and disease. No, we trust in the Lord for our protection and safety. Through His Word, we bolster our faith in His desire and ability to protect us. God is our refuge!

May you not be afraid *for the Lord* is your shield (Gen. 15:1b, NIV).

May your pleas for deliverance *from the things that threaten you or enslave you* rise up to God (Exod. 2:23b, NLT).

May you *find rest and peace in knowing* the Lord keeps vigil for *His chosen ones. May you likewise* keep vigil to honor the Lord (Exod. 12:42, NIV).

May the Lord *be your* Banner, *Jehovah Nissi* (Exod. 17:15, NIV).

May the Divine Presence of the Lord be with you. May the Lord rise up! May His enemies be scattered; may His foes flee before *Him* (Num. 10:35, NIV).

May God give you rest from all your enemies around you so that you live in security (Deut. 12:10, NASB).

May God make you strong and bold, may you not be afraid or frightened of *the unknown, nor of risks, nor of your enemies, nor the enemies of God*, for Adonai your God goes with you. He will neither fail you nor abandon you (Deut. 31:6, CJB).

May the Lord protect you, care for you, and guard you like the pupil of His eye, as an eagle that stirs up her nest, hovers over her young, spreads out her wings, takes them, and carries them as she flies (Deut. 32:10b-11, CJB).

May the Lord repay your work and may a full reward be given you by the Lord God of Israel, under whose wings you have come for refuge (Ruth 2:12, NKJV).

Blessings for God's Protection & Safety

May the Lord protect you…His godly one(s) (1 Sam. 2:9a, NLT).

The Lord is your rock and your fortress and your deliverer; *may you confidently know like King David, He* is the God of your strength, in whom you can trust; He is your shield and the horn of your salvation; He is your stronghold and your refuge (2 Sam. 22:2b-3, NKJV).

May the Lord lead you to a place of safety; He rescues you because He delights in you (2 Sam. 22:20, NLT).

May you know that God's way is perfect; may you know the Word of the Lord is flawless. May the Lord be a shield to you as you take refuge in Him (2 Sam. 22:31, NIV).

May you *walk in the knowledge and constant reality that there* is no God, besides the Lord. Who is a rock, besides our God? (2 Sam. 22:32, NASB).

May you *always have confidence that* God is your strength and your protection; He makes your way straight (2 Sam. 22:33, CJB).

May God make you as surefooted as a deer, leading you safely along the mountain heights. *If God calls you to a place of apparent risk or danger, He will protect you, despite what the situation appears to be* (2 Sam. 22:34 & Ps. 18:33, NLT).

May God be a tower of salvation to you and may He show mercy to *you*…His anointed one (2 Sam. 22:51, NKJV).

May God open your eyes so you can see *the resources He has dispatched to meet your need* (2 Kings 6:17, KJV).

May God bless you and enlarge your territory! May the hand of God be with you and keep you from harm so that you will be free from pain (1 Chron. 4:10b, NIV).

May you have faith in the Lord your God, and may you stand strong (2 Chron. 20:20, NCV).

When you cry out to the Lord, may He hear you from heaven and may He deliver you many times according to His mercies (Neh. 9:28, NKJV).

May you be confident because there is hope *in the Lord*. May you look around yourself and lie down in security *because the Lord is your protector*. May you rest because no one *can* make you afraid (Job 11:18-19a, CJB).

You are blessed, who trust the Lord for protection (Ps. 2:12, NCV).

May the Lord be a shield for you; your glory, and the lifter of your head (Ps. 3:3, KJV).

May God, who saves the upright in heart, be your shield (Ps. 7:10, CJB).

May the Lord be a refuge for you in times of oppression, your stronghold in times of trouble. Because you know the name of the Lord, you can confidently put your trust in Him, for the Lord has never forsaken those who seek Him (Ps. 9:9-10, NIV).

May God keep you as the apple of His eye, and may He hide you under the shadow of His wings (Ps. 17:8, KJV).

May the Lord be your rock and your fortress and your deliverer; He is your God, your strength, in whom you can trust; your shield and the horn of your salvation, your stronghold (Ps. 18:2, NKJV).

May the Lord answer you in the day of trouble; may the name of the God of Jacob defend you (Ps. 20:1, NKJV).

May the Lord send thee help from His sanctuary, and strengthen thee out of Zion (Ps. 20:2, KJV).

May the Lord prepare a table before you in the presence of your enemies, *even in the midst of oppression, tribulation, or fear* (Ps. 23:5a, KJV).

Be blessed in knowing the Lord is your light and your salvation; whom therefore shall you fear? *Be blessed in knowing* the Lord is the strength of your life; of whom shall you be afraid? (Ps. 27:1, KJV).

In the day of trouble, may God keep you safe in His dwelling; may He hide you in the shelter of His tabernacle and may He set you high upon a rock (Ps. 27:5, NIV).

May the Lord be your hiding place. May He protect you from your troubles and fill you with songs of salvation (Ps. 32:7, NCV).

May the angel of the Lord encamp all around you and deliver you *because you* fear God (Ps. 34:7, NKJV).

May the children of men put their trust under the shadow of Thy wings (Ps. 36:7b, KJV).

May the Lord save *you*; He is your strength in times of trouble. May the Lord help you and save you; may He save you from the wicked because you trust in Him for protection (Ps. 37:39-40, NCV).

May the Lord protect you and keep you alive, and you shall be called blessed upon the earth. May the Lord not give you over to the desire of your enemies (Ps. 41:2, NASB).

May God be your refuge and strength, an ever-present help in trouble. Therefore may you not fear, though the earth give way and the mountains fall into the heart of the sea, though its waters roar and foam and the mountains quake with their surging (Ps. 46:1-3, NIV).

May the Lord show you *His* favor and *may you know you can* go to Him for safety. May you find safety in the shadow of His wings and may you stay there until the danger is gone (Ps. 57:1, NIrV).

May you *confidently know that God* only is your rock and your salvation; He is your defense; so that you shall not be moved (Ps. 62:6, NKJV).

May your honor and salvation come from God. He is your mighty rock and your protection (Ps. 62:7, NCV).

May the Lord be for you a rock of refuge to which you can always go. His command saves you, for He is your rock and your fortress (Ps. 71:3, NIV).

May you dwell in the secret place of the most High and *may you* abide under the shadow of the Almighty (Ps. 91:1, KJV).

May the Lord cover you with His feathers, and under His wings may you find refuge; His faithfulness will be your shield and rampart (Ps. 91:4, NIV).

May the Lord give His angels charge over you, to keep you in all your ways. In their hands may they bear you up, lest you dash your foot against a stone (Ps. 91:11-12, NKJV).

May the Lord deliver you because you have loved Him; may the Lord set you securely on high because you have known His name (Ps. 91:14, NASB).

May the Lord answer you when you call upon Him and may He be with you when you are in trouble. May He deliver you and bring you honor (Ps. 91:15, NIV).

May the Lord rescue your soul from death, your eyes from tears, and your feet from stumbling (Ps. 116:8, NASB).

May the Lord be your hiding place and your shield. May you put your hope in His Word (Ps. 119:114, NKJV).

May your help come from the Lord, maker of heaven and earth (Ps. 121:2, CJB).

May the Lord, your Rock, train you for war. *It is He who* trains you for battle. May He protect you like a strong, walled city; *may you never doubt how much* He loves you. May He be your defender and your Savior, your shield and your protection (Ps. 144:1-2a, NCV).

May you walk securely because you walk in integrity (Prov. 10:9a, TNIV).

May the name of the Lord be a strong tower *for you; as His* righteous *one*, you may run to it and *be* safe (Prov. 18:10, NIV).

May the Lord make you today as a fortified city and as a pillar of iron and as walls of bronze (Jer. 1:18a, NASB).

May the Lord be your strength, your fortress, and your refuge in the day of affliction (Jer. 16:19a, KJV).

May you know how good it is to wait quietly for salvation from the Lord (Lam. 3:26, NLT).

May the Lord, who is good, be *your* stronghold in the day of trouble; He knows those who trust in Him (Nah. 1:7, NKJV).

May the Lord your God, as a victorious warrior, *be* in your midst...*at all times...no matter where you may be.* He will *rejoice* over you with joy, He will be quiet in His love *for you*, He will rejoice over you with shouts of joy (Zeph. 3:17, NASB).

May you be empowered by the grace that comes from Jesus our Savior (2 Tim. 2:1, CJB).

II
Blessings for God's Provision

But if God so clothes the grass of the field,
which is alive today
and tomorrow is thrown into the furnace,
will He not much more clothe you?
~ Matthew 6:30 (NASB) ~

Consider the ravens, for they neither sow nor reap,
which have neither storehouse nor barn; and God feeds
them. Of how much more value are you than the birds?
~ Luke 12:24 (KJV) ~

God has a flawless track record of providing for His people. After Adam and Eve committed the first sin, He provided animal skins to cover their nakedness. He provided an ark to rescue Noah and his family. Every morning for forty years, the Lord provided manna for the children of Israel as they wandered in the wilderness.

Jesus mentored His followers about trusting the heavenly Father for all their provision. Our Savior Himself made the greatest contribution to mankind when He provided redemption for our sins and gave us everlasting life. Whether physical, mental, spiritual, financial or basic material needs, Jehovah Jireh, our provider, is the source for everything we need.

May God give you of heaven's dew and of earth's richness – an abundance of grain and new wine (Gen. 27:28, NIV).

May the Lord be with you and may He make you to prosper in whatever you do (Gen. 39:23b, CJB).

May the Lord, the God of your fathers, increase you a thousand-fold more than you are and bless you, just as He has promised you (Deut. 1:11, CJB).

May the Lord your God bless you in all your harvest and in all the work of your hands, and may your joy be complete (Deut. 16:15, NIV).

May the Lord open for you His good storehouse, the heavens, to give rain to your land in its season and to bless all the work of your hand (Deut. 28:12a, NASB).

May the Lord make you strong and be pleased with the work you do (Deut. 33:11, NCV).

May you be blessed as you are faithful not to let the Book of the Law depart from your mouth. *May you be faithful to* meditate on it day and night so that you will be careful to do everything written in it. Then you will be prosperous and successful (Josh. 1:8, NIV).

May you be very careful to keep the commandment and the law that Moses the servant of the Lord gave you: to love the Lord you God, to walk in all His ways, to obey His commands, to hold fast to Him and to serve Him with all your heart and all your soul. As you go on your life journey and are faithful to do these things, may you return with great wealth (Josh. 22:5 & 8, NIV).

May the Lord repay your work and may a full reward be given you by the Lord God of Israel, under whose wings you have come for refuge (Ruth 2:12, NKJV).

May God give you new life and take care of you in your old age (Ruth 4:15a, NCV).

May God bless you and enlarge your territory! May the hand of God be with you and keep you from harm so that you will be free from pain (1 Chron. 4:10b, NIV).

May God open your eyes so you can see *the resources He has dispatched to meet your need* (2 Kings 6:17, KJV).

May the Lord give rain on the earth and send water on the fields (Job 5:10, NASB).

May your future be so prosperous, your beginnings will seem humble (Job 8:7, NIV).

May you sing to the Lord because He gives you more than you need (Ps. 13:6, CJB).

Because the Lord is your shepherd, you shall not want (Ps. 23:1, KJV).

May God cause you to live in prosperity, and may your children inherit the Promised Land (Ps. 25:13, NLT).

May you feast on the abundance of God's house; may He give you drink from His river of delights (Ps. 36:8, NIV).

May the Lord our God treat you well. May He give you success in what you do; yes, give you success in what you do (Ps. 90:17, NCV).

May God veil the sky with clouds above you and may He provide the earth with rain. May He cause grass to grow on the hills and may He give food to the animals, even to the young ravens when they cry (Ps. 147:8-9, CJB).

As you honor the Lord with your wealth and give Him the first share of all your income, may your storerooms be so full they can't hold everything (Prov. 3:9-10a, NIrV).

The blessing of the Lord makes *you* rich, and He adds no sorrow with it (Prov. 10:22, NKJV).

May you prosper and be satisfied *as you are* generous *to others*; those who refresh others will themselves be refreshed (Prov. 11:25, NLT).

May God give you the ability to enjoy the wealth and property He gives you. May He also give you the ability to accept your state in life and enjoy your work (Eccles. 5:19, NCV).

May the Lord pour water out on your thirsty land. May He make streams flow on your dry ground (Isa. 44:3a, NIrV).

May the Lord give you the treasures of darkness and hidden wealth of secret places, so that you may know that it is the Lord, the God of Israel, who calls you by your name (Isa. 45:3, NASB).

May the Lord build you using fairness. May you be safe from those who would hurt you, so you will have nothing to fear. Nothing can come to make you afraid (Isa. 54:14, NCV).

May the Lord satisfy you with abundance and may you be filled with His bounty (Jer. 31:14, TNIV).

May God be your inheritance: God Himself is your possession (Ezek. 44:28, KJV).

May you flourish like grain and blossom like grapevines. May you be as fragrant as the wines of Lebanon. *May you be confident that the Lord is the one who looks after you, cares for you, and causes you to flourish* (Hosea 14:7, NLT).

May you know the Lord is the one who answers your prayers and watches over you. He is like a green pine tree; your blessings come from Him. A wise person will know these things, and an understanding person will take them to heart (Hosea 14:8b-9a, NCV).

As you bring your whole tithe into the storehouse that there may be food in the Lord's house, may God throw open the floodgates of heaven and pour out so much blessing that you will not have room enough for it (Mal. 3:10, NIV).

May you seek first the kingdom of God and His righteousness and all *the* things *you need* shall be added unto you (Matt. 6:33, KJV).

May He who supplies seed to the sower and bread for food, supply and multiply the seed you have sown and increase the fruits of your righteousness (2 Cor. 9:10, NKJV).

May you be enriched in everything for all liberality (*openhandedness*), which causes thanksgiving through you to God (2 Cor. 9:11, NKJV).

May God supply all your need according to His riches in glory by Christ Jesus (Phil. 4:19, KJV).

May you prosper in all things and be in health, just as your soul prospers (3 John 1:2, NKJV).

12
Blessings over Family

*Behold, children are a gift of the Lord,
the fruit of the womb is a reward.*
~ Psalm 127:3 (NASB) ~

*Husbands, love your wives,
even as Christ also loved the Church,
and gave Himself for it.*
~ Ephesians 5:25 (KJV) ~

Families are the precious design of the Lord. He calls us His children and calls Himself our Abba, Father. God created woman so that man would not be alone. Marriage is the powerful symbol He used to help us understand the relationship between Jesus, the bridegroom and the Church, His bride.

The Lord set the example of blessing His "bride" and His "children." Just as God blessed families throughout the Bible, we must be faithful to bless our spouses, children, families, and extended families.

For Entire Families

May God Almighty bless you and make you fruitful and multiply you that you may become a company of many peoples (Gen. 28:3, CJB).

May *the Lord* give you and your descendants the blessing given to Abraham, so that you may take possession of *all He has promised you* (Gen. 28:4, NIV).

May the Lord bless you and keep you; may the Lord make His face shine upon you, and be gracious to you; may the Lord lift up His countenance upon you, and give you peace (Num. 6:24-26, NKJV).

May you eat your offerings in the presence of the Lord. May you rejoice over everything you set out to do in which the Lord your God has blessed you, you and your household (Deut. 12:7, CJB).

After you have brought the first fruits of the *provision* which the Lord has given you, and you have set it before the Lord your God, and worshiped before the Lord your God, *may you then* rejoice in every good thing which the Lord your God has given to you and your house (Deut. 26:10a-11a, NKJV).

May the Lord bless you from Zion; may you see the prosperity of Jerusalem all the days of your life (Ps. 128:5, TNIV).

May your house be built by wisdom and may understanding make it secure (Prov. 24:3, NIrV).

For Parents

May your house be like *the tribe of Judah* through the offspring which the Lord will give you (*has given you*) (Ruth 4:12b, NASB).

May God cause you to live in prosperity, and may your children inherit the Promised Land (Ps. 25:13, NLT).

May the Lord cause you to increase, both you and your children (Ps. 115:14, TNIV).

Children are a gift from the Lord; they are a reward from Him. How *blessed* is the *one* whose quiver is full of them (Ps. 127:3 & 5a, NLT).

May you live to see your children's children (Ps. 128:6, TNIV).

May your sons in their youth be like well-nurtured plants, and may your daughters be like pillars carved to adorn a palace (Ps. 144:12, NIV).

May you *develop a* strong confidence in your fear of the Lord, and may your children have refuge (Prov. 14:26, NASB).

May your children be blessed because you *received* the righteousness *of Christ that permitted you to* be *found* blameless (Prov. 20:7, TNIV).

May God pour out His Spirit on your children. May He pour out His blessing on their children after them. May they spring up like grass in a meadow and may they grow like poplar trees near flowing streams (Isa. 44:3b-4, NIrV).

May all your children be taught by the Lord and may your children have great peace (Isa. 54:13, NKJV).

May *your children* be without defect, may they be good-looking, showing intelligence in every branch of wisdom, *may they be* endowed with understanding and discerning knowledge, and *may they have* the ability for serving in the court of the King *of Kings* (Dan. 1:4, NASB).

May God *give your* children knowledge and skill in all learning and wisdom. May they have understanding in all visions and dreams (Dan. 1:17, KJV).

For Husbands & Fathers

Blessed is the man who fears the Lord, who greatly delights in His commandments! His descendants will be mighty in the land; the generation of the upright will be blessed. Wealth and riches are in his house; and his righteousness endures forever. Light rises in the darkness for the upright; *for* the Lord is gracious, merciful, and righteous. It is well with the man who deals generously and lends, who conducts his affairs with justice. For the righteous will never be moved; he will be remembered forever. He is not afraid of evil tidings; his heart is firm, trusting in the Lord. His heart is steady, he will not be afraid. He distributes freely, he gives to the poor; his righteousness endures forever; *and* his *life* is exalted in honor (Ps. 112:1-9, RSV). *Note:* This is the traditional Sabbath eve blessing spoken by the wife over her husband.

This is how the man who respects the Lord will be blessed: you will enjoy what you work for and you will be blessed with good things. Your wife will give you many children, like a vine that produces much fruit.

Your children will bring you much good, like olive branches that produce many olives (Ps. 128:2-4, NCV).

For Wives & Mothers

Who can find a virtuous wife? For her worth is far above rubies. The heart of her husband safely trusts her; so he will have no lack of gain. She does him good and not evil all the days of her life. She extends her hand to the poor, yes, she reaches out her hands to the needy. Strength and honor are her clothing; she shall rejoice in time to come. She opens her mouth with wisdom, and on her tongue is the law of kindness. Her children rise up and call her blessed; her husband also, and he praises her: "Many daughters have done well, but you excel them all" (Prov. 31:10-12, 20, 25-26, 28-29, NKJV). *Note:* This is the traditional Sabbath eve blessing spoken by the husband over his wife.

For Sons

May God make you like Ephraim and Manasseh (Gen. 48:20, CJB). *Note:* This is the traditional Sabbath eve blessing spoken by parents over their sons.

May you be strong and prove yourself a man. May you keep the charge of the Lord your God: to walk in His ways, to keep His statutes, His commandments, His judgments, and His testimonies, as it is written in the Law of Moses, that you may prosper in all that you do and wherever you turn (1 Kings 2:2-3, NKJV).

For Daughters

May the Lord make you like Rachel and Leah, who had many children and built up the people of Israel (Ruth

4:11b, NCV). *Note:* This is the traditional Sabbath eve blessing spoken by parents over their daughters.

May *the Lord make you like Esther, may you* find favor and kindness with the King *of Kings* (Esther 2:17, NASB).

13
Blessings for God's Children

But ye are a chosen generation, a royal priesthood, an holy nation, a peculiar people; that ye should shew forth the praises of Him who hath called you out of darkness into His marvelous light.
~ 1 Peter 2:9 (KJV) ~

But if some of the branches were broken off, and you, being a wild olive, were grafted in among them and became partaker with them of the rich root of the olive tree, do not be arrogant toward the branches; but if you are arrogant, remember that it is not you who supports the root, but the root supports you.
~ Romans 11:17-18 (NASB) ~

What an awesome privilege…God chose us! He adopted us into His family. Having been grafted into the tree of Israel, we share in the same covenant He made with Abraham the patriarch. We may legitimately call the King of the entire universe our "Abba, Father." He delights in us, His children. As we allow His Holy Spirit to internalize these truths within us, we will begin to live with the confidence and humility of heirs to the Eternal Sovereign. We can then embrace our calling to live sanctified lives and walk in the power and victory for which we are destined.

Note: Chapter 27 is devoted specifically to Blessings over Israel

May you be set apart to dedicate the most holy things *for God*, to offer sacrifices in the Lord's presence, to serve the Lord, and to pronounce blessings in His name forever (1 Chron. 23:13, NLT).

May your farms be filled with crops of every kind. May the flocks in your fields multiply by the thousands, even tens of thousands, and may your oxen be loaded down with produce. May there be no breached walls, no forced exile, and no cries of distress in your squares. Yes, happy are those who have it like this! Happy indeed are those whose God is the Lord (Ps. 144:13-15, NLT).

May the Lord take pleasure in you: He will beautify the meek with salvation (Ps. 149:4, KJV).

The righteous has an everlasting foundation, *established by the Lord* (Prov. 10:25b, NASB).

May you *know the Lord sees you, His bride,* like the sunrise in all of its glory. You are to Him as beautiful as the moon, as bright as the sun, as majestic as troops carrying their banners (Song of Sol. 6:10, NIrV).

May *Jesus the Bridegroom* set you as a seal upon His heart, as a seal upon His arm (Song of Sol. 8:6a, NKJV).

May the Lord be like dew to you. May you blossom like a lily and may you take root like the cedars of Lebanon. May your branches spread out, may your beauty be like an olive tree and may your fragrance be like the cedars of Lebanon (Hosea 14:5-6, CJB).

May *the lost, hurting people you encounter* grasp *your* sleeve and say, "Let us go with you, for we have heard that God is with you" (Zech. 8:23, NKJV).

I commend you to God and to the Word of His grace, which is able to build you up and to give you an inheritance among all them which are sanctified (Acts 20:32, KJV).

May you *be confident that you are* God's son/daughter because you are being led by His Spirit. *May you embrace and walk in the reality that* you did not receive the spirit of slavery to fall back into fear, but you have received the spirit of sonship (Rom. 8:14-15b, RSV).

May God keep you strong to the very end so *that* you will be without blame on the day our Lord Jesus Christ returns. God is faithful. He has chosen you to share life with His Son, Jesus Christ our Lord (1 Cor. 1:8-9, NIrV).

May you have boldness and confident access *to God* through faith in Christ Jesus, in accordance with the eternal purpose which God the Father carried out in Christ Jesus our Lord (Eph. 3:11-12, NASB).

May you joyfully give thanks to the Father, who has qualified you to share in the inheritance of the saints in the kingdom of light (Col. 1:11c-12, NIV).

You are a chosen generation, a royal priesthood, a holy nation, a peculiar people; that *you* should show forth the praises of Him who hath called you out of darkness into His marvelous light (1 Pet. 2:9, KJV).

14
Blessings about Confrontation

*For we wrestle not against flesh and blood,
but against principalities, against powers,
against the rulers of the darkness of this world,
against spiritual wickedness in high places.*
~ Ephesians 6:12 (KJV) ~

*Yet in all these things we are more than conquerors
through Him who loved us.*
~ Romans 8:37 (KJV) ~

If we are alive and breathing, then we are probably facing a struggle. Life in a sin-plagued world is not always a walk in the park. At times, it can seem as though we move from one problem to another. Often we cause our own troubles. Some of life's challenges are circumstantial; others are direct attacks from the enemies of God who hate us because we are His children. We encounter criticism, obstacles, and challenges throughout our earthly journey.

But Jesus told us in John 16:33, *"In the world you have tribulation, but take courage; I have overcome the world"* (NASB). The Scriptures assure us that we serve the King of Kings. He is in control of the entire universe and He is prepared to defend us against the challenges we confront.

May God make you strong and bold, may you not be afraid of *the unknown, nor of risks, nor of your enemies nor the enemies of God,* for Adonai your God goes with you. He will neither fail you nor abandon you (Deut. 31:6, CJB).

May the Lord hearken unto your voice and may He fight on your behalf (Josh. 10:14, KJV).

May your life be valued much in the eyes of the Lord and may He deliver you out of all tribulation (1 Sam. 26:24, NKJV).

May the Lord lead you to a place of safety; He rescues you because He delights in you (2 Sam. 22:20, NLT).

May the Lord train your hands for battle, so that your arms can bend a bow of bronze. *He equips you for any challenge or confrontation, that by the strength of Him who is your source, you will be able to do the impossible* (2 Sam. 22:35, NASB).

May God open your eyes so you can see *the resources He has dispatched to meet your need* (2 Kings 6:17, KJV).

May you be strong and courageous. May you not be afraid or discouraged because of the *obstacles, issues, or spiritual battles confronting you,* for there is a greater power with *you* than with *any force opposing you.* The Lord *your* God is with *you* to help *you* and to fight *your* battles. May you gain confidence *from this truth* (2 Chron. 32:7-8, NIV).

As you look over your situation, may you not be afraid of *whoever or whatever appears to be a threat to you*! Remember the Lord, who is great and glorious, and *do spiritual warfare* for your friends, your families, and your homes (Neh. 4:14, NLT).

May the Lord be a refuge for you in times of oppression, your stronghold in times of trouble. Because you know the name of the Lord, you can confidently put your trust in Him, for the Lord has never forsaken those who seek Him (Ps. 9:9-10, NIV).

May the Lord train your hands for battle; may your arms *be able to* bend a bow of bronze. *Because God is the One who has called you, He will enable you to achieve results beyond any level you think to be possible* (Ps. 18:34, TNIV).

May the Lord prepare a table before you in the presence of your enemies, *even in the midst of oppression, tribulation, or fear* (Ps. 23:5a, KJV).

May you hold your head higher than your enemies around you. May you offer joyful sacrifices in God's Holy Tent. May you sing and praise the Lord (Ps. 27:6, NCV).

May the Lord protect you and keep you alive, and you shall be called blessed upon the earth. May the Lord not give you over to the desire of your enemies (Ps. 41:2, NASB).

May God give you victory. You will succeed because of the Lord's mighty power; you will succeed because He favors you and smiles on you (Ps. 44:3, NLT).

May God send from heaven and save you, rebuking those who hotly pursue you; may God send you His love and His faithfulness (Ps. 57:3, NIV).

May you put your trust in the Lord: may He never allow you to be put to confusion. He will deliver you in His righteousness and cause you to escape *whatever threatens you*. May the Lord incline His ear unto you and save you (Ps. 71:1-2, KJV).

Blessed is the man whom the Lord corrects. Blessed is the person God teaches from His law. He gives him rest from times of trouble (Ps. 94:12-13a, NIrV).

Though you walk in the midst of trouble, the Lord will revive you. May He stretch forth His hand against the wrath of your enemies and may His right hand save you (Ps. 138:7, NASB).

May the Lord make even your enemies to be at peace with you (Prov. 16:7b, KJV).

May God go before you and make the rough places smooth; may He shatter the doors of bronze and cut through their iron bars (Isa. 45:2, NASB).

May the Lord make *you like* a fire and a flame *so that you can* set *to* fire and consume the *obstacles, temptations, and challenges that hinder you* (Obad. 1:18, NIV).

May you look to the Lord and may you wait for the God of your salvation *knowing He* will hear you. Your enemy will not rejoice over you because when you fall, you will arise *with the help of almighty God, the Lord of Hosts*; when you sit in darkness, the Lord will be a light to you (Mic. 7:7-8, NKJV).

May you be strong in the Lord and in the power of His might. May you put on the whole armor of God that *you* may be able to stand against the wiles of the devil. For we wrestle not against flesh and blood, but against principalities, against powers, against the rulers of the darkness of this world, against spiritual wickedness in high places (Eph. 6:10-12, KJV).

May you take up the whole armor of God that you may be able to withstand in the evil day, and having done all, *you will be able* to stand (Eph. 6:13, NKJV).

May you be strengthened with all power according to God's glorious might so that you may have great endurance and patience (Col. 1:11, NIV).

15
Blessings for Courage

*Be strong and courageous.
Do not be afraid or terrified because of them,
for the Lord your God goes with you;
He will never leave you nor forsake you.*
~ Deuteronomy 31:6 (TNIV) ~

*The Lord is my strength and my shield;
my heart trusts in Him, and I am helped; therefore
my heart exults, and with my song I shall thank Him.*
~ Psalm 28:7 (NASB) ~

When we allow ourselves to get caught up in our emotions, we can become timid, fearful, or weak-willed. Sometimes our obligations seem overwhelming. We feel responsible for so many things and people are depending on us. Pride can deceive us into fearing we "have to go it alone." We may doubt ourselves.

Perhaps you are intimidated about sharing the Good News of salvation. Maybe you were raised in a home that deprived you of affirmation; you may sincerely believe you can't do anything. You may feel worthless or lack confidence.

As we submit ourselves to God's power and authority, our strength is bolstered. We can grow to accept the reality that we "*can do all things through Christ who strengthens us*" (Phil. 4:13). When we build our faith through immersion in these truths…we also build courage.

May you not be afraid *for the Lord* is your shield (Gen. 15:1b, NIV).

May God make you strong and bold, may you not be afraid of *the unknown, nor of risks, nor of your enemies nor the enemies of God*, for Adonai your God goes with you. He will neither fail you nor abandon you (Deut. 31:6, CJB).

May the Lord train your hands for battle, so that your arms can bend a bow of bronze. *He equips you for any challenge or confrontation, that by the strength of Him who is your source, you will be able to do the impossible* (2 Sam. 22:35, NASB).

May the Lord make a wide path for your feet to keep them from slipping. *May you allow God to stretch you out of your comfort zone. Be confident He will not allow you to fail* (2 Sam. 22:37 & Ps. 18:36, NLT).

May you be strong and courageous *as you set out to accomplish the* work *God has called you to do*. May you not be afraid or discouraged, for the Lord God…*your* God, is with you. He will not fail you or forsake you until all your work for *His* service is finished (1 Chron. 28:20, NIV).

May you be strong and not let your hands be weak, for your work shall be rewarded (2 Chron. 15:7, NKJV).

May you take courage as you fulfill your duties and may the Lord be with *you as you* do what is right (2 Chron. 19:11b, NLT).

May you become mighty because you prepare your ways before the Lord your God (2 Chron. 27:6, KJV).

May you be strong and courageous. May you not be afraid or discouraged because of the *obstacles, issues, or spiritual battles confronting you*, for there is a greater power with *you* than with *any force opposing you*. The Lord *your* God is with *you* to help *you* and to fight *your* battles. May you gain confidence *from this truth* (2 Chron. 32:7-8, NIV).

May you be strengthened according to the hand of the Lord your God upon you (Ezra 7:28b, NASB).

As you look over your situation, may you not be afraid of *whoever or whatever appears to be a threat to you!* Remember the Lord, who is great and glorious, and *do spiritual warfare* for your friends, your families, and your homes (Neh. 4:14, NLT).

May the joy of the Lord be your strength (Neh. 8:10, KJV).

May God arm you with strength; He has made your way safe (Ps. 18:32, NLT).

Be blessed in knowing the Lord is your light and your salvation; whom therefore shall you fear? *Be blessed in knowing* the Lord is the strength of your life; of whom shall you be afraid? (Ps. 27:1, KJV).

May you be of good courage and may the Lord strengthen your heart as you hope *in Him* (Ps. 31:24, KJV).

May the angel of the Lord encamp all around you and deliver you *because you* fear God (Ps. 34:7, NKJV).

May God be your refuge and strength, an ever-present help in trouble. Therefore may you not fear, though the earth give way and the mountains fall into the heart of the sea, though its waters roar and foam and the mountains quake with their surging (Ps. 46:1-3, NIV).

May you *have abundant happiness because* your strength is in the Lord and in your heart are pilgrim highways *to His Holy Mountain.* May you go from strength to strength and appear before God in Zion (Ps. 84:5&7, CJB).

Behold, God is your salvation, may you trust *in Him* and not be afraid; for the Lord God is your strength and song, and He has become your salvation. Therefore may you joyously draw water from the springs of salvation (Isa. 12:2-3, NASB).

May calmness and confidence in the Lord make you strong (Isa. 30:15b, CJB).

May the Lord be gracious to you as you wait for Him. May He be your arm every morning, your salvation also in the time of trouble (Isa. 33:2, NKJV).

As you wait upon the Lord, may you renew your strength; may you mount up with wings as eagles; may you run and not be weary; and may you walk and not faint (Isa. 40:31, KJV).

May you not be afraid for the Lord is with you; may you not be dismayed for the Lord is your God. May He strengthen you, may He help you, and may He uphold you with His righteous right hand (Isa. 41:10, NKJV).

May the Lord your God take hold of your right hand and may you hear Him say to you, "Do not fear; I will help you" (Isa. 41:13, TNIV).

May the Lord build you using fairness. May you be safe from those who would hurt you, so you will have nothing to fear. Nothing can come to make you afraid (Isa. 54:14, NCV).

May the Spirit of the Lord make you brave (Mic. 3:8c, NIrV).

May the sovereign Lord be your strength! May He make you as surefooted as a deer and may He bring you safely over the mountains (Hab. 3:19, NLT).

May you take courage in the Lord of Hosts and be about His work for He is with you (Hag. 2:4, CJB).

May you *remember* the promise God made you when you came out of *your past life of sin*. His Spirit is abiding *with you* (in your midst) *therefore* do not fear (Hag. 2:5, NASB).

May you take heart; trust God and believe that what He has said will come true (Acts 27:25, CJB).

May the preaching of the cross be the power of God unto you (1 Cor. 1:18, KJV).

May the eyes of your understanding be enlightened so that you may know the hope of God's calling, *so that you may know* the riches of the glory of His inheritance, and *so that you may know* the exceeding greatness of His power toward *you as you* believe according to the working of His mighty power (Eph. 1:18-19, NKJV).

May God, out of His glorious riches, strengthen you with power through His Spirit in your inner being, so that Christ may dwell in your heart through faith (Eph. 3:16-17a, NIV).

May you be strong in the Lord and in the power of His might. May you put on the whole armor of God that *you* may be able to stand against the wiles of the devil. For we wrestle not against flesh and blood, but against principalities, against powers, against the rulers of the darkness of this world, against spiritual wickedness in high places (Eph. 6:10-12, KJV).

May you be strengthened with all power according to God's glorious might so that you may have great endurance and patience (Col. 1:11, NIV).

16
Blessings about Destiny & Calling

Where there is no vision, the people perish.
~ Proverbs 29:18 (KJV) ~

*"For I know the plans I have for you," declares the Lord,
"plans for welfare and not for calamity,
to give you a future and a hope."*
~ Jeremiah 29:11 (NASB) ~

From Genesis through Revelation, the Scriptures speak about destiny and calling. The Creator instills a desire in the human soul to dream dreams and set goals. It is the excellence of God's character in us that gives us the drive to press diligently toward the finish line. The Lord births the desire in us for achievement and success. The Bible convincingly affirms how the Lord equips us – His children – to live our lives with significance for Him, for others, and for ourselves.

May the Lord, the God of Abraham, let you succeed today and show His grace to you (Gen. 24:12, CJB).

May the Lord *be* with *you* and *may He give* you success in whatever *you do* (Gen. 39:23b, NIV).

May the Lord endow you with the wisdom to carry out every assignment He has given you (Exod. 31:6, CJB).

May the *Lord* send an angel ahead of you to guard you along *your* way and *may He* bring you to the place He has prepared *for you* (Exod. 23:20, NIV).

May you be strong and very courageous; may you be careful to do according to all the law of Moses. *May you be faithful to God's Word and* not turn from it to the right or to the left, so that you may have success wherever you go (Josh. 1:7, NASB).

May you be *consciously aware that* God has given you the shield of His salvation; His help makes you great (2 Sam. 22:36, NASB).

May the Lord be with you and may you prosper (1 Chron. 22:11b, NKJV).

May you be set apart to dedicate the most holy things *for God*, to offer sacrifices in the Lord's presence, to serve the Lord, and to pronounce blessings in His name forever (1 Chron. 23:13, NLT).

May the Lord enable you to successfully accomplish all that *He has put* in your heart (2 Chron. 7:11b, NKJV).

May you *accomplish things that are* good and right and truthful before the Lord your God (2 Chron. 31:20, KJV).

In every project you undertake in the service of God's *house* and in obedience to the law and the commands, may you seek God wholeheartedly. As a result, *you will be* very successful *in fulfilling His purposes for you* (2 Chron. 31:21 NLT).

May the God of heaven give you success; therefore as His servant, may you arise and *set about doing His work with confidence (*Neh. 2:20, NASB).

May your future be so prosperous, your beginnings will seem humble (Job 8:7, NIV).

May God do all He has planned for you. He controls your destiny (Job 23:14, NLT).

May the Lord, who has given you the shield of His salvation, uphold you with His right hand; may His gentleness make you great (Ps. 18:35, NASB).

May the Lord grant you your heart's desire and bring all your plans to success (Ps. 20:4, CJB).

May God, the Most High, accomplish His purpose for you (Ps. 57:2, CJB).

May the Lord accomplish what concerns you; the lovingkindness of the Lord is everlasting (Ps. 138:8a, NASB).

May you *always walk* in righteousness, *knowing that your God-given authority, power, and influence* are made secure by righteousness (Prov. 16:12b, CJB).

May you be confident of this very thing, that He who has begun a good work in you will complete it until the day of Jesus Christ (Phil. 1:6, NKJV).

17
Blessings for Encouragement

Nevertheless I tell you the truth;
It is expedient for you that I go away:
for if I go not away,
the Comforter will not come unto you;
but if I depart, I will send him unto you.
~ John 16:7 (NKJV) ~

For everything that was written in the past
was written to teach us, so that through endurance
and the encouragement of the Scriptures
we might have hope.
~ Romans 15:4 (NIV) ~

We serve the living, Eternal God who is our solid rock, our sure foundation. As we absorb what the Bible has to say about the all-powerful, all-loving, enduring nature of God, our spirits resonate with comfort and hope. The Scriptures are a rich source of encouragement that our heavenly Father truly cares for us.

May the Lord bless you and keep you; may the Lord make His face shine upon you, and be gracious to you; may the Lord lift up His countenance upon you, and give you peace (Num. 6:24-26, NKJV).

May the Lord protect you, care for you, and guard you like the pupil of His eye, as an eagle that stirs up her nest, hovers over her young, spreads out her wings, takes them, and carries them as she flies (Deut. 32:10b-11, CJB).

May you be like the morning light at dawn, like a morning without clouds. May you be like sunshine after a rain that makes the grass sprout from the ground (2 Sam. 23:4, NCV).

May God gently call you from the jaws of trouble to an open place of freedom where He has set your table full of the best food (Job 36:16, NCV).

May God lead you in His truth and teach you, for He is the God of your salvation; may you wait on Him all the day (Ps. 25:5, NKJV).

When the troubles of your heart are enlarged, may the Lord bring you out of your distresses (Ps. 25:17, NASB).

May you taste and see that the Lord is good: blessed is the man that trusteth in Him (Ps. 34:8, KJV).

May the Lord put a new song in your mouth, a song of praise to our God. Many people will see this and worship Him. Then they will trust the Lord (Ps. 40:3, NCV).

May your soul wait in silence for God only, for your hope is from Him (Ps. 62:5, NASB).

May your help come from the Lord, maker of heaven and earth (Ps. 121:2, CJB).

May you wait longingly for the Lord. May you put your hope in His Word (Ps. 130:5, CJB).

May the Lord turn your mourning into gladness; may He give you comfort and joy instead of sorrow (Jer. 31:13b, NIV).

May you recall this to mind and may you therefore have hope: the Lord's lovingkindnesses indeed never ceases, for His compassions never fail. They are new every morning; great is His faithfulness (Lam. 3:21-23, NASB).

May you say to yourself, "The Lord is everything I will ever need. So I will put my hope in him" (Lam. 3:24, NIrV).

I commend you to God and to the Word of His grace, which is able to build you up and to give you an inheritance among all those who are sanctified (Acts 20:32, KJV).

May God keep you strong to the very end so *that* you will be without blame on the day our Lord Jesus Christ returns. God is faithful. He has chosen you to share life with His Son, Jesus Christ our Lord (1 Cor. 1:8-9, NIrV).

May the God of peace make you holy in every way, and may your whole spirit and soul and body be kept blameless until that day when our Lord Jesus Christ comes again. God, who calls you, is faithful; He will do this (1 Thess. 5:23-24, NLT).

May our Lord Jesus Christ Himself and God our Father encourage you and strengthen you in every good thing you do and say. God loves you, and through His grace He gave you a good hope and encouragement that continues forever (2 Thess. 2:16-17, NCV).

May you put your hope in the living God, who is the Savior of all men, and especially of those who believe (1 Tim. 4:10b, NIV).

May your confidence in both the promise and oath of God be like a strong and trustworthy anchor for your soul. These two things are unchangeable because it is impossible for God to lie (Heb. 6:18-19a, NLT).

18

Blessings for Godly Character

*The Lord has sought out for Himself
a man after His own heart,
and the Lord has appointed him
as ruler over His people.*
~ 1 Samuel 14:3b (NASB) ~

*Finally, brethren, whatever is true, whatever is honorable,
whatever is right, whatever is pure, whatever is lovely,
whatever is of good repute, if there is any excellence and
if anything is worthy of praise, dwell on these things.*
~ Philippians 4:8 (NASB) ~

Wholeheartedness before the Lord is a powerful Biblical theme. It is the essential quality God expects from His followers. David figured it out. He was a man after God's own heart. We may outwardly express obedience to God through our words and deeds but God knows our hearts are the true source of our motives.

As the Apostle Paul understood, nothing good dwells in us naturally. Our conformance to the ways of God is a transformation process that requires our active participation. We must choose to take on the character of Christ by applying His Word and heeding the voice of His Holy Spirit within us.

May you worship the Lord your God (Exod. 23:25a, NIV).

May you be strong and very courageous; may you be careful to do according to all the law of Moses. *May you be faithful to God's Word and* not turn from it to the right or to the left, so that you may have success wherever you go (Josh. 1:7, NASB).

May your love for the Lord *make you radiant* like the sun when it comes out in full strength (Judg. 5:31b, NKJV).

May the Lord protect you…His godly one(s) (1 Sam. 2:9a, NLT).

May you *always have confidence that* God is your strength and your protection; He makes your way straight (2 Sam. 22:33, CJB).

May you live righteously. *May you be blessed with righteous thoughts, words, and deeds and* may you always fear God (2 Sam. 23:3, NASB).

May you be strong and prove yourself a man. May you keep the charge of the Lord your God: to walk in His ways, to keep His statutes, His commandments, His judgments, and His testimonies, as it is written in the Law of Moses, that you may prosper in all that you do and wherever you turn (1 Kings 2:2-3, NKJV).

May you set your heart and your soul to seek the Lord your God (1 Chron. 22:19, KJV).

May you be set apart to dedicate the most holy things *for God*, to offer sacrifices in the Lord's presence, to serve the Lord, and to pronounce blessings in His name forever (1 Chron. 23:13, NLT).

May you *have the character of* a gatekeeper in the house of the Lord. May you be a strong, brave man/woman, a valiant man/woman of ability and strength for service (1 Chron. 26:1,6-8, CJB).

May you serve God with a whole heart and a willing mind; for the Lord searches all hearts, and understands every intent of the thoughts. If you seek Him, He will let you find Him (1 Chron. 28:9, NASB).

May you be full of joy as you covenant, with all your heart and with all your being, to put to death *those behaviors, thoughts, and attitudes in your life* that refuse to seek the Lord God. May you be full of joy because of this oath you make with all your heart and because you seek Him with all your will; you will find Him and He will give you rest all around (2 Chron. 15:12-13, 15, CJB).

May your heart be blameless all your days (2 Chron. 15:17, NASB).

May you serve faithfully and wholeheartedly in the fear of the Lord (2 Chron. 19:9, NIV).

May you take courage as you fulfill your duties and may the Lord be with *you as you* do what is right (2 Chron. 19:11b, NLT).

May you serve God, *His people*, and your household well (2 Chron. 24:16b, CJB).

May you become mighty because you prepare your ways before the Lord your God (2 Chron. 27:6, KJV).

May the hand of God give you one heart *with others in His kingdom* to do *what your leaders have directed* by the Word of the Lord (2 Chron. 30:12, KJV).

In every project you undertake in the service of God's *house* and in obedience to the law and the commands, may you seek God wholeheartedly. As a result, *you will be* very successful *in fulfilling His purposes for you* (2 Chron. 31:21 NLT).

May the Lord *help you commit what He desires from you:* to stand in your place, to make a covenant before the Lord to walk after the Lord; to keep His commandments and His testimonies and His statutes, with all your heart and with all your soul, to perform the words of the covenant which are written in *His Word* (2 Chron. 34:31, KJV).

May you *walk with the integrity of godly royalty, caring not what man thinks, but obeying what God speaks to your heart (*Esther 4:16)

May you *be blessed with a heart that causes you to* seek the good of your people and may you become one who speaks for the welfare of his *family / community / church* / nation (Esther 10:3, NASB).

Blessed are those who don't listen to the wicked, who don't go where sinners go, and who don't do what evil people do (Ps. 1:1, NCV).

The Lord blesses the godly, surrounding them with His shield of love (Ps. 5:12, NLT).

May you *truly know that* God establishes the just; for the righteous God tests the hearts and minds *to know those who have been made righteous through Christ Jesus.* Your defense is of God, who saves the upright in heart (Ps. 7:9-10, NKJV).

Blessings for Godly Character

May you be blessed for living a blameless life, for behaving uprightly, for speaking truth from your heart and keeping your tongue from slander, for never doing harm to others or seeking to discredit your neighbors (Ps. 15:2-3, CJB).

Blessed are you for honoring those who honor the Lord and for keeping your promises to your neighbors, even when it hurts (Ps. 15:4, NCV).

May you *have a healthy fear of the Lord and receive the blessing of all those who fear Him.* May the Lord instruct you in the way *He has* chosen for you (Ps. 25:12, NIV).

May integrity and uprightness preserve you as you wait for the Lord (Ps. 25:21, NKJV).

May all those who seek the Lord rejoice and be glad in Him; may those who love God's salvation say continually, "Let God be magnified!" (Ps. 70:4, NKJV).

May you *have abundant happiness because* your strength is in the Lord and in your heart are pilgrim highways *to His Holy Mountain. May your influence be* like one passing through the dry desert, making it a place of springs and like the early rains, clothing it with blessings. May you go from strength to strength and appear before God in Zion (Ps. 84:5-7, CJB).

May *the righteousness of Christ in you cause you to* flourish like a palm tree. May you grow like a cedar of Lebanon. May you be planted in the house of the Lord and flourish in the courts of our God (Ps. 92:12-13, TNIV).

Blessed are those who keep justice and those who do righteousness at all times (Ps. 106:3, NKJV).

The Lord will bless those who fear Him, both great and small (Ps. 115:13, NLT).

Blessed are they whose ways are blameless, who walk according to the law of the Lord (Ps. 119:1, NIV).

Blessed are those who keep *the* testimonies *of God*, who seek Him with *their* whole heart! They also do no iniquity; they walk in His ways (Ps. 119:2-3, NKJV).

May the Lord do good unto those *who are* good and to *those who* are upright in their hearts: *those who have become the righteousness of God in Christ Jesus* (Ps. 125:4, 2 Cor. 5:21, KJV).

May you walk *in* the way of good people and keep to the paths of the righteous (Prov. 2:20, CJB).

May you walk securely because you walk in integrity (Prov. 10:9a, TNIV).

As you sow righteousness may you reap a sure reward: the truly righteous man attains life (Prov. 11:18b-19a, NIV).

May the Lord examine your motives and find your ways to be pure (Prov. 16:2, NLT).

May you *always walk* in righteousness, *knowing that your God-given authority, power, and influence* are made secure by righteousness (Prov. 16:12b, CJB).

May you fear God and keep His commandments (Eccles. 12:13b, KJV).

May goodness and fairness give you strength, like a belt around your waist (Isa. 11:5, NCV).

May respect for the Lord be your greatest treasure (Isa. 33:6b, NCV).

May you listen to the commands *of God*! Then you will have peace flowing like a gentle river and righteousness rolling like waves. (*Waves never stop, neither should our obedience to God cease*) (Isa. 48:18, NLT).

May the Lord your Savior and your Redeemer, the Mighty One of *Israel* make peace your administrators and righteousness your overseers (Isa. 60:16b & 17b, NASB).

May you be *like Daniel*, determined to understand and to humble yourself before your God, confident that your words have been heard *by Him* (Dan. 10:12, CJB).

May you sow for yourself righteousness, *so that you will* reap in mercy. May you break up your fallow ground (*unproductive, idle places in your life*), for it is time to seek the Lord, till He comes and rains righteousness on you (Hosea 10:12, NKJV).

May the Spirit of the Lord fill you with power and may He help you do what is fair (Mic. 3:8a, NIrV).

May your soul magnify the Lord and may your spirit rejoice in God, your Savior (Luke 1:46, NKJV).

May the source of your life be Christ Jesus, whom God has made our wisdom, our righteousness, our sanctification and our redemption (1 Cor. 1:30, RSV).

May your spirit and mind keep being renewed and may you clothe yourself with the new nature created to be godly, which expresses itself in the righteousness and holiness that flow from the Truth (Eph. 4:23-24, CJB).

May you be filled with the fruit of righteousness which *comes* through Jesus Christ, to the glory and praise of God (Phil. 1:11, NASB).

May you be a blameless and innocent *child* of God, without blemish in the midst of a crooked and perverse generation, among whom you *will* shine as *a* light in the world, *as you* hold fast the Word of Life (Phil. 2:15-16a, RSV).

May you live a life worthy of the Lord and please Him in every way: bearing fruit in every good work and growing in the knowledge of God (Col. 1:10, TNIV).

As you have therefore received Christ Jesus the Lord, may you walk in Him, rooted and built up in Him and established in the faith as you have been taught, abounding in it with thanksgiving (Col. 2:6-7, NKJV).

May you lead a quiet and peaceable life in all godliness and honesty (1 Tim. 2:2, KJV).

May the Lord cause you to increase and abound in love for all people, so that He may establish your heart without blame in holiness before our God and Father at the coming of our Lord Jesus with all His saints (1 Thess. 3:12-13, NASB).

May the God of peace make you holy in every way, and may your whole spirit and soul and body be kept blameless until that day when our Lord Jesus Christ comes again. God, who calls you, is faithful; He will do this (1 Thess. 5:23-24, NLT).

May *your reputation be of* your love and faith which you have toward the Lord Jesus and toward all the saints (Philem. 1:5, NKJV).

May you be an imitator of those who, through faith and patience, inherit what has been promised *by the Lord* (Heb. 6:12b, NIV).

May you *be a diligent seeker of God and trust that* He is a rewarder of them that diligently seek Him (Heb. 11:6, KJV).

In everything you say and do, may you remember that you will be judged by the Law that makes people free (James 2:12, NCV).

May God's divine power give you everything you need for life and godliness through your knowledge of Him who called you by His own glory and goodness. Through these He has given you His very great and precious promises, so that through them you may participate in the divine nature and escape the corruption in the world caused by evil desires (2 Pet. 1:3-4, NIV).

May you buy from the Lord gold refined in the fire (*things of enduring, eternal value*), that you may be rich; and white garments (*the redemption of Jesus' blood that washes our sins away*), that you may be clothed, that the shame of your nakedness (*sin and guilt*) may not be revealed; and *may you* anoint your eyes with eye salve (*spiritual discernment*), that you may see (Rev. 3:18, NKJV).

19
Blessings for Godly Speech

*A gentle answer turns away wrath,
but a harsh word stirs up anger.*
~ Proverbs 15:1 (NASB) ~

*Like apples of gold in settings of silver
is a word appropriately spoken.*
~ Proverbs 12:11 (CJB) ~

Our words can affirm others or condemn them. We can either speak words of life or words of death. Speech is a powerful tool that we must develop to be used for good, not evil. As ambassadors of God, our language should reflect His love, His wisdom and knowledge, and His message of redemption and hope. We have the ability to communicate the value our Father has placed in each and every person.

Each time we open our mouths, we are given the opportunity to say something that will bless and not curse. We can have an impact on ungodliness in our society with the things we say. May we be a beacon for the Lord by allowing Him to shine forth through the words we speak.

May *God* help you speak and teach you what to do (Exod. 4:15, NIV).

May your *Godly instruction be valuable* to many people and may your strength be a help to those with weak hands. May your words comfort those who have fallen, and may you strengthen those who cannot stand (Job 4:3-4, NCV).

May *the Lord anoint* your words to give life, like a fountain of water (Prov. 10:11a, NCV).

May you speak what is right and may it be of value to others (Prov. 16:13b, TNIV).

May the wisdom of your heart teach your mouth *what to say* and may it add learning to your lips (Prov. 16:23, NKJV).

May the knowledge your lips speak *be received with the value* of a rare jewel (Prov. 20:15b, TNIV).

May you speak the right words at the right time and may they be as beautiful as gold apples in a silver bowl (Prov. 25:11, NCV).

May the Lord God give you the ability to teach so that you *will* know what to say to make the weak strong (Isa. 50:4a, NCV).

May the Lord put His words in your mouth and may He cover you with the shadow of His hand (Isa. 51:16a, NKJV).

How beautiful upon the mountains are the feet of *those* who bring good news, who proclaim peace, who bring glad tidings of good things, who proclaim salvation, who say to Zion, "Your God reigns!" (Isa. 52:7, NKJV).

May you powerfully refute *all skepticism and resistance raised against God*, demonstrating by the Scriptures that Jesus *is* the Christ (Acts 18:28, NASB).

May you *walk in* the grace God has given you in Christ Jesus. May you be made rich in every way, in all your speaking and in all your knowledge (1 Cor. 1:4-5, NCV).

Speaking the truth in love, may *you* grow up into Him in all things, which is the head, even Christ (Eph. 4:15, KJV).

May the Word of Christ dwell in you richly in all wisdom *as you* teach and admonish *others* in psalms and hymns and spiritual songs, singing with grace in your heart to the Lord (Col. 3:16, KJV).

May you keep speaking and acting like a person who will be judged by the *Law* which gives freedom (James 2:12, CJB).

20
Blessings for Healing & Long Life

Bless the Lord, O my soul,
And forget not all His benefits:
Who forgives all your iniquities,
Who heals all your diseases.
~ Psalm 103:2-3 (NKJV) ~

With a long life I will satisfy him
and let him see My salvation.
~ Psalm 91:16 (NASB) ~

We all desire health and longevity, for our loved ones and for ourselves. We belong to the One who created us and has the power to heal. Our heavenly Father is the giver of life. The woman with the issue of blood knew that if she merely touched the hem of the Master's robe, she would be healed (Matthew 9:21-22). We want to bless others so they can reach out to God and experience His healing, life-giving power.

May you *be strengthened by the truth that God is* the Lord who heals you (Exod. 15:26, NIV).

May you worship the Lord your God, and may His blessing be on your food and water (*the things you need for survival*). *May the Lord* take away sickness from among you (Exod. 23:25, NIV).

May your strength match the length of your days (Deut. 33:25b, NLT).

May you *live a long life*, may your eyes be undimmed and may your vigor be undiminished (Deut. 34:7, CJB).

May God give you new life and take care of you in your old age (Ruth 4:15a, NCV).

May you live to be a good old age, full of days and riches and honor (1 Chron. 29:28, NKJV).

May the Lord strengthen you on your bed of illness; may He sustain you on your sickbed (Ps. 41:3, NKJV).

May the Lord deliver you from death and *may He keep* your feet from stumbling, so that you may walk before God in the light of life (Ps. 56:13, TNIV).

May the Lord satisfy you with a long life and give you His salvation (Ps. 91:16, NLT).

May *the righteousness of Christ in you cause* you to flourish like a palm tree. May you grow like a cedar of Lebanon. May you be planted in the house of the Lord and flourish in the courts of our God. May you still bear fruit in old age, staying fresh and green, and proclaiming, "The Lord is upright; He is my Rock, and there is no wickedness in Him" (Ps. 92:12-15, TNIV).

May the Lord forgive all your iniquities and may He heal all your diseases (Ps. 103:3, NKJV).

May the Lord satisfy your desires with good things so that your youth is renewed like the eagle's (Ps. 103:5, NIV).

May the Lord rescue your soul from death, your eyes from tears, and your feet from falling (Ps. 116:8, CJB).

May you walk before the Lord in the land of the living (Ps. 116:9, KJV).

May the Lord bless you from Zion; may you see the prosperity of Jerusalem all the days of your life. May you live to see your children's children (Ps. 128:5-6, TNIV).

May you not forget *God's* teaching, but may you keep His commands in mind; then you will live a long time, and your life will be successful (Prov. 3:1-2, NCV).

May you fear the Lord and shun evil. This will bring health to your body and nourishment to your bones (Prov. 3:7b-8, TNIV).

May the *wisdom* and sayings of God be life to you and health to your flesh (Prov. 4:22, NKJV).

May you be healthy like a green leaf (Prov. 11:28, NCV).

May the fear of the Lord be a fountain of life to you, enabling you to depart from the snares of death (Prov. 14:27, KJV).

May *the Lord* strengthen your tired hands and encourage your weak knees (Isa. 35:3, NLT).

May the Lord give strength to you *when you are* weary and may He increase your power *when you are* weak (Isa. 40:29, NIV).

As you wait upon the Lord, may you renew your strength; may you mount up with wings as eagles; may you run and not be weary; and may you walk and not faint (Isa. 40:31, KJV).

May God bring you health and healing. May He heal you and reveal to you an abundance of peace and truth (Jer. 33:6, NASB).

For you who fear *the* name *of the Lord*, the Sun of Righteousness will rise with healing in His wings and you will go free, leaping with joy like calves let out to pasture (Mal. 4:2, NLT).

May the Lord be moved with compassion for you *and may He* heal *you from your* sickness (Matt. 14:14, NKJV).

May you prosper in all things and be in health, just as your soul prospers (3 John 1:2, NKJV).

21
Blessings for Joy

*These things I have spoken to you
so that My joy may be in you,
and that your joy may be made full.*
~ John 15:11 (NASB) ~

*For the kingdom of God is not food and drink
but righteousness and peace and joy in the Holy Spirit.*
~ Romans 14:17 (RSV) ~

God expresses joy in all three persons of the Godhead and He wants us to have joy. Happiness may be a demonstration of joy but it does not fully describe the extent of joy. There was heavenly rejoicing over the act of creation. The shepherd in the parable rejoiced in the recovery of His lost sheep. Jesus, the author and finisher of our faith, endured the cross for the joy that was set before Him. Fullness of joy results from being in God's will. The Scriptures remind us that our heavenly Father is the source of true joy, contentment, and happiness.

May the Lord your God bless you in all your harvest and in all the work of your hands, and may your joy be complete (Deut. 16:15, NIV).

After you have brought the first fruits of the *harvest* which the Lord has given you, and you have set it before the Lord your God, and worshiped before the Lord your God, *may you then* rejoice in every good thing which the Lord your God has given to you and your house (Deut. 26:10a-11a, NKJV).

May you rejoice when *you* have offered willingly to the Lord, because with perfect heart *you* offered willingly to Him. May *you* rejoice with great joy (1 Chron. 29:9a, KJV).

May the Lord God make you, His priest, to be clothed with salvation, and may you rejoice in the goodness of the Lord (2 Chron. 6:41b, NLT).

May you be full of joy as you covenant, with all your heart and with all your being, to put to death *those behaviors, thoughts, and attitudes in your life* that refuse to seek the Lord God. May you be full of joy because of this oath you make with all your heart and because you seek Him with all your will; you will find Him and He will give you rest all around (2 Chron. 15:12-13, 15, CJB).

May the joy of the Lord be your strength (Neh. 8:10, KJV).

May the Lord turn your sorrow into joy and your mourning into a day of celebration (Esther 9:22b, TNIV).

May the Lord yet fill your mouth with laughter and your lips with shouts of joy (Job 8:21, NLT).

As you take refuge in the Lord, may you be glad and may you ever sing for joy. May the Lord spread His protection over you that you who love His name may rejoice in Him (Ps. 5:11, NIV).

May you set the Lord continually before you; because He is at your right hand, you will not be shaken. Therefore may your heart be glad and may your glory rejoice; may your flesh also will dwell securely (Ps. 16:8-9, NASB).

May the Lord show you the path of life. In His presence is fullness of joy and at His right hand are pleasures forevermore (Ps. 16:11, NKJV).

May the Lord turn your mourning into dancing! May He remove your sackcloth and clothe you with joy (Ps. 30:11, CJB).

May the Lord put a new song in your mouth, a song of praise to our God. Many people will see this and worship Him. Then they will trust the Lord (Ps. 40:3, NCV).

May all those who seek the Lord rejoice and be glad in Him; may those who love God's salvation say continually, "Let God be magnified!" (Ps. 70:4, NKJV).

May you find happiness in what the Lord has done. May you take joy in what His hands have made (Ps. 92:4, CJB).

May you sing unto the Lord as long as you live: may you sing praise to God while you have your being.

May your meditation of Him be sweet and may you be glad in the Lord (Ps. 104:33-34, KJV).

May you glory in the Holy Name of the Lord; may your heart be glad because you seek Him (Ps. 105:3, NASB).

Blessed are all who fear the Lord, who walk in His ways (Ps. 128:1, NIV).

The blessing of the Lord makes *you* rich, and He adds no sorrow with it (Prov. 10:22, NKJV).

May your righteous hope *result in* gladness (Prov. 10:28a, KJV).

May wisdom make your face shine (Eccles. 8:1b, NKJV).

May your delight be in the fear of the Lord (Isa. 11:3a, NKJV).

May the Lord console you when you mourn, giving you beauty for ashes, the oil of joy for mourning, the garment of praise for the spirit of heaviness; that you may be called a tree of righteousness, the planting of the Lord, that He may be glorified (Isa. 61:3, NKJV).

May you delight greatly in the Lord; may your soul rejoice in your God. For He has clothed you with garments of salvation and arrayed you in a robe of righteousness, as a bridegroom adorns his head like a priest, and as a bride adorns herself with her jewels (Isa. 61:10, NIV).

May you come home and sing songs of joy on the heights of Jerusalem (Jer. 31:12, NLT).

May the Lord turn your mourning into gladness; may He give you comfort and joy instead of sorrow (Jer. 31:13b, NIV).

May you rejoice in the Lord and may you be joyful in God your Savior, *even* though the fig tree does not blossom and there be no fruit on the vines, *even though* the yield of the olive should fail and the fields produce no food, *even* though the flock *may* be cut off from the fold and there be no cattle in the stalls (Hab. 3:17-18, NASB).

May you rejoice in the Lord and may you take joy in the God of your salvation (Hab. 3:18, CJB).

May your soul magnify the Lord and may your spirit rejoice in God, your Savior (Luke 1:46, NKJV).

May the God of hope fill you with all joy and peace in believing, that you may abound in hope, through the power of the Holy Ghost (Rom. 15:13, KJV).

May you joyfully give thanks to the Father, who has qualified you to share in the inheritance of the saints in the kingdom of light (Col. 1:11c-12, NIV).

22

Blessings for Anointing in Ministry

*Then He said to them,
"Follow Me, and I will make you fishers of men."*
~ Matthew 4:19 (NKJV) ~

For the gifts and calling of God are irrevocable.
~ Romans 11:29 (NASB) ~

Jesus relied on the anointing and empowerment of His heavenly Father to accomplish His earthly mission. How much more do we need the infusion of the Holy Spirit to give meaning and substance to our ministries? We serve as emissaries of the Most High everywhere we go…in our homes, workplaces, schools, and communities.

We may be ministering to the masses or we may simply be placing a hand on the shoulder of a broken friend who needs the peace of God. Whatever it is the Lord may call us to do, we can only be effective in ministry if we serve under His anointing.

May the oil of God's anointing be upon you (Lev. 10:7, CJB).

May you be like the morning light at dawn, like a morning without clouds. May you be like sunshine after a rain that makes the grass sprout from the ground (2 Sam. 23:4, NCV).

May the Word of the Lord be with you (2 Kings 3:12, KJV).

May you be set apart to dedicate the most holy things *for God*, to offer sacrifices in the Lord's presence, to serve the Lord, and to pronounce blessings in His name forever (1 Chron. 23:13, NLT).

May you *have the character of* a gatekeeper in the house of the Lord. May you be a strong, brave man/woman, a valiant man/woman of ability and strength for service (1 Chron. 26:1,6-8, CJB).

May you be strong and courageous *as you set out to accomplish the* work *God has called you to do*. May you not be afraid or discouraged, for the Lord God…*your* God, is with you. He will not fail you or forsake you until all your work for *His* service is finished (1 Chron. 28:20, NIV).

May you serve God, *His people*, and your household well (2 Chron. 24:16b, CJB).

In every project you undertake in the service of God's *house* and in obedience to the law and the commands, may you seek God wholeheartedly. As a result, *you will be* very successful *in fulfilling His purposes for you* (2 Chron. 31:21 NLT).

May *your commitment* to walk in covenant relationship with the Lord and wholeheartedly obey His Word *encourage others to stand with you in* affirming their covenant with God (2 Chron. 34:31-32, CJB).

May you set your heart to study the law of the Lord and to practice it and to teach His statutes and ordinances (Ezra 7:10, NASB).

May the God of heaven give you success; therefore as His servant, may you arise and *set about doing His work with confidence* (Neh. 2:20, NASB).

May you work with all your heart *because you are doing the work of the Lord* (Neh. 4:6, NIV).

May you be blessed with a heart that causes you to seek the good of your people and may you become one who speaks for the welfare of your *family / community / church /* nation (Esther 10:3, NASB).

May your *Godly instruction be valuable* to many people and may your strength be a help to those with weak hands. May your words comfort those who have fallen, and may you strengthen those who can not stand (Job 4:3-4, NCV).

May the Lord anoint your head with oil and may your cup runneth over (Ps. 23:5b, KJV).

May your *desire and your life-long search be focused on the eternal things of God.* May you dwell in the house of the Lord all the days of your life, to behold the beauty of the Lord, and to enquire in His temple (Ps. 27:4, KJV).

Blessed is the one who cares about weak people. When he is in trouble, the Lord saves him (Ps. 41:1, NIrV).

May the Lord's endowment of justice and righteousness *cause you to* be like rain falling on a mown field, like showers watering the earth. *May you be His representative of replenishment and life* (Ps. 72:1 & 6, TNIV).

The fruit of the righteous is a tree of life; and he that winneth souls is wise (Prov. 11:30, KJV).

May your cheerful look bring joy to the hearts *of others* and may your good news give health to *their* bones (Prov. 15:30, NIV).

May the light of your face be life *to others because you convey the Spirit of the Lord.* May your favor be like a cloud with the spring rain *so others will recognize that God's Spirit brings hope and renewal* (Prov. 16:15, NASB).

May your trustworthiness as a messenger refresh those who send you, like the coolness of snow in the summertime (Prov. 25:13, NCV).

May the Spirit of the Lord rest on you – the Spirit of wisdom and understanding, the Spirit of counsel and might, the Spirit of knowledge and of the fear of the Lord (Isa. 11:2, NKJV).

May your news *of the Lord's coming,* displayed *in* glory and splendor, strengthen those who have tired hands and encourage those who have weak knees (Isa. 35:2b-3, NLT).

May the Lord God give you the ability to teach so that you *will* know what to say to make the weak strong. May He wake you every morning and may He teach you to listen like a student (Isa. 50:4, NCV).

How beautiful upon the mountains are the feet of *those who bring good news, who proclaim peace, who bring glad tidings of good things, who proclaim salvation, who say to Zion, "Your God reigns!"* (Isa. 52:7, NKJV).

May the Spirit of the Lord God be upon you (Isa. 61:1, KJV).

May the Lord satisfy you, His priest, with abundance and may you be filled with His bounty (Jer. 31:14, TNIV).

As the Lord teaches you, *may your words and your actions demonstrate to others* the difference between the Holy and the profane, and cause them to discern between the unclean and the clean (Ezek. 44:23, KJV).

May God be your inheritance: God Himself is your possession (Ezek. 44:28, KJV).

May God give you understanding in all visions and dreams (Dan. 1:17b, KJV).

May God make you wise and may you shine like the brightness of the sky. May you lead many others to do what is right and may you be like the stars forever and ever (Dan. 12:3, NIrV).

May your feet bring good tidings and proclamations of peace...*everywhere you go* (Nah. 1:15a, NKJV).

May *the lost and hurting people you encounter* grasp *your* sleeve and say, "Let us go with you, for we have heard that God is with you" (Zech. 8:23, NKJV).

May you *always be* a rich, *fertile soil, ready to receive the life containing seed that is the Word of God*. May His Word sprout in you, grow, and yield a bountiful harvest...30,

60, and even 100 times what He has sown and will sow in you (Mark 4:8, CJB).

May you be blessed with ears that listen *and may you understand the Word of the Lord* (Mark 4:9, NIrV).

May the hand of the Lord be with you, and may a great number of people trust and turn to the Lord *because you allowed God to work through you* (Acts 11:21, CJB).

May the testimony of Christ be confirmed in you and may you not lack any spiritual gift as you eagerly wait for our Lord Jesus Christ to be revealed (1 Cor. 1:6-7, NIV).

As you serve the Lord with your brothers and sisters in Christ, may you agree with one another so that there may be no divisions among you and may you be perfectly united in mind and thought *through God's Spirit* (1 Cor. 1:10, NIV).

May you know and understand that your competence is from God. He has made you competent to be a worker serving a New Covenant, the essence of which is not a written text but the Spirit (2 Cor. 3:5-6, CJB).

May He who supplies seed to the sower and bread for food, supply and multiply the seed you have sown and increase the fruits of your righteousness (2 Cor. 9:10, NKJV).

May the Word of Christ dwell in you richly in all wisdom *as you* teach and admonish *others* in psalms and hymns and spiritual songs, singing with grace in your heart to the Lord (Col. 3:16, KJV).

May the kindness and love of God our Savior *be revealed to others through you* (Titus 3:4, KJV).

May the God of peace equip you with everything good *so* that you may do His will; working in you that which is pleasing in His sight, through Jesus Christ (Heb. 13:20-21, RSV).

23
Blessings for Peace, Rest & Patience

*Peace I leave with you; My peace I give to you;
not as the world gives do I give to you.
Do not let your heart be troubled, nor let it be fearful.*
~ John 14:27 (NASB) ~

*There remains then a Sabbath-rest
for the people of God.*
~ Hebrews 4:9 (NIV) ~

God Himself rested after the six days of creation. He established the pattern for what He formally instituted as the Sabbath ("Shabbat" in Hebrew) in the book of Exodus. The Lord wants us to rest and He wants us to rest in Him. He is the Prince of Peace; the Author of Peace.

Peace and patience are fruit of the spirit (Gal. 5:22), meaning we innately possess them as believers. Our challenge is to walk in them. As we discipline ourselves to follow God's ways and allow Him to bestow His benefits upon us, we become less affected by our circumstances. We may find ourselves in the midst of tribulation, but we can still know peace because the God of the universe is working on our behalf. The Lord will give us patience as we wait on Him to fulfill His eternal plan.

May you *find rest and peace in knowing* the Lord keeps vigil for *His chosen ones. May you likewise* keep vigil to honor the Lord (Exod. 12:42, NIV).

May the Lord bless you and keep you; may the Lord make His face shine upon you, and be gracious to you; may the Lord lift up His countenance upon you, and give you peace (Num. 6:24-26, NKJV).

May God make you as surefooted as a deer, leading you safely along the mountain heights (2 Sam. 22:34 & Ps. 18:33, NLT).

Peace, peace to you, and peace to him who helps you; indeed, your God helps you (1 Chron. 12:18, NASB).

May you be a man / woman of rest (1 Chron. 22:9b, KJV).

May you be full of joy as you covenant, with all your heart and with all your being, to put to death *those behaviors, thoughts, and attitudes in your life* that refuse to seek the Lord God. May you be full of joy because of this oath you make with all your heart and because you seek Him with all your will; you will find Him and He will give you rest all around (2 Chron. 15:12-13, 15, CJB).

May you be confident because there is hope *in the Lord*. May you look around yourself and lie down in security *because the Lord is your protector*. May you rest because no one *can* make you afraid (Job 11:18-19a, CJB).

In peace may you lie down and sleep, for God alone makes you to dwell in safety (Ps. 4:8, NASB).

May you *know with confidence* that you will never be moved from your place of rest in the tent of the Lord or from life on His holy mountain (Ps. 15:1, CJB).

May the Lord make you to lie down in green pastures, may He lead you beside still waters (Ps. 23:2, KJV).

May the Lord give *you* strength; may the Lord bless *you* with His peace (Ps. 29:11, NKJV).

May you be still in the presence of the Lord and wait patiently for Him to act (Ps. 37:7a, NLT).

May your soul wait in silence for God only, for your hope is from Him (Ps. 62:5, NASB).

May our heavenly Father give sleep to you, His beloved (Ps. 127:2b, KJV).

May you not be afraid when you lie down and may your sleep be sweet (Prov. 3:24, CJB).

May the Lord make even your enemies to be at peace with you (Prov. 16:7b, KJV).

May the Lord keep you in perfect peace *because your* mind is stayed on *God* and because you trust in *Him* (Isa. 26:3, NKJV).

May the work of righteousness *in your life* be peace; may the effect of righteousness *in your life* be quietness and assurance forever (Isa. 32:17, KJV).

May you listen to the commands *of God*! Then you will have peace flowing like a gentle river and righteousness rolling like waves. (*Waves never stop, neither should our obedience to God cease*) (Isa. 48:18, NLT).

May the Lord your Savior and your Redeemer, the Mighty One of *Israel* make peace your administrators and righteousness your overseers (Isa. 60:16b & 17b, NASB).

May God bring you health and healing. May He heal you and reveal to you an abundance of peace and truth (Jer. 33:6, NASB).

May you be blessed with grace and peace from God our Father, and the Lord Jesus Christ (Rom. 1:7b, KJV).

May the God of hope fill you with all joy and peace in believing, that you may abound in hope, through the power of the Holy Ghost (Rom. 15:13, KJV).

May grace be unto you, and peace, from God our Father, and from the Lord Jesus Christ (1 Cor. 1:3, KJV).

May you be blessed with grace and peace from God the Father and from our Lord Jesus Christ, who gave Himself for our sins, that He might deliver us from this present evil world, according to the will of God our Father (Gal. 1:3-4, KJV).

May you be blessed with peace and love with faith from God the Father and the Lord Jesus Christ. Grace to you who love our Lord Jesus Christ with love that never ends (Eph. 6:23-24, NCV).

May the peace of God, which surpasses all understanding, guard your heart and mind through Christ Jesus (Phil. 4:7, NKJV).

May you be strengthened with all power according to God's glorious might so that you may have great endurance and patience (Col. 1:11, NIV).

May grace, mercy, and peace *be yours* from God the Father and Christ Jesus our Lord (1 Tim. 1:2b, NCV).

May you lead a quiet and peaceable life in all godliness and honesty (1 Tim. 2:2, KJV).

May grace and peace be multiplied unto you through the knowledge of God, and of Jesus our Lord (2 Pet. 1:2, KJV).

24
Blessings for Faith & Trust

*Trust in the Lord always,
for the Lord God is the eternal Rock.*
~ Isaiah 26:4 (NLT) ~

*And without faith it is impossible to please Him,
for he who comes to God must believe that He is,
and that He is a rewarder of those who seek Him.*
~ Hebrews 11:6 (NASB) ~

By faith we trust in Jesus as our Redeemer and Lord. Faith is the means by which we accept many of the things we receive from God. It is the act of believing what God says is true.

In our journey through life, we are constantly required to trust God for what we cannot see. How do we know Jesus rose from the dead? How do we know we have an eternal future in a place called heaven? How do we know the Lord will provide food and shelter for us during our unemployment? How do we know God will heal our sick child? How do we know He hears our prayers?
By trust. By faith.

Our confidence in His unseen intervention is strengthened as we spend time in His Word. The more we know Him, the more the Holy Spirit impresses upon us...what God says...He will do.

May you have faith in the Lord your God, and may you stand strong (2 Chron. 20:20, NCV).

Because you know the name of the Lord, you can confidently put your trust in Him, for the Lord has never forsaken those who seek Him (Ps. 9:10, NIV).

May you have trust in God's mercy and may your heart rejoice in your salvation (Ps. 13:5, KJV).

May the Lord plant your feet on level ground (Ps. 26:12a, CJB).

Blessed are those who make the Lord their trust, who do not look to the proud, to those who turn aside to false gods (Ps. 40:4, TNIV).

As you trust in the Lord, may you be like Mount Zion, which cannot be moved but abides forever (Ps. 125:1, NASB).

May you trust in the Lord with all your heart and lean not on your own understanding; in all your ways submit to Him, and He will make your paths straight (Prov. 3:5-6, TNIV).

May the Lord keep you in perfect peace *because your* mind is stayed on *God* and because you trust in *Him* (Isa. 26:3, NKJV).

Blessed are you as you trust in the Lord; may your hope be in the Lord. May you be like a tree planted by the waters, which spreads out its roots by the river, and will not fear when heat comes; but its leaf will be green, and it will not be anxious in the year of drought, nor will it cease from yielding fruit (Jer. 17:7-8, NKJV).

The Lord knows the plans He has for you, plans for welfare and not for calamity to give you a future and a hope. *May you embrace this truth* – when you call upon the Lord and pray to Him, He will listen to you. You will seek the Lord and find Him when you search for Him with all your heart (Jer. 29:11-13, NASB).

The Lord is good to those whose hope is in Him, to the one who seeks Him (Lam. 3:25, TNIV).

May you be *like Daniel*, determined to understand and to humble yourself before your God, confident that your words have been heard (Dan. 10:12, CJB).

May the God of hope fill you with all joy and peace in believing, that you may abound in hope, through the power of the Holy Ghost (Rom. 15:13, KJV).

May your faith not stand in the wisdom of men, but in the power of God (1 Cor. 2:5, KJV).

May you *confidently* receive, not the spirit of the world, but the Spirit who is from God, that you might know the things that have been freely given to you by God (1 Cor. 2:12, NKJV).

May you be blessed with peace and love with faith from God the Father and the Lord Jesus Christ. Grace to you who love our Lord Jesus Christ with love that never ends (Eph. 6:23-24, NCV).

May you be confident of this very thing, that He who has begun a good work in you will complete it until the day of Jesus Christ (Phil. 1:6, NKJV).

May your confidence in both the promise and oath of God be like a strong and trustworthy anchor for your soul. These two things are unchangeable because it is impossible for God to lie (Heb. 6:18-19a, NLT).

May you draw near to God with a sincere heart in full assurance of faith, having your heart sprinkled clean from an evil conscience and *having* your body washed with pure water. May you hold fast the confession of your hope without wavering, for He who promised is faithful (Heb. 10:22-23, NASB).

May you rejoice in a living hope through the resurrection of Jesus Christ from the dead. In all this you may greatly rejoice, though now for a little while you may have had to suffer grief in all kinds of trials. These have come so that your faith – of greater worth than gold, which perishes even though refined by fire – may be proved genuine and may result in praise, glory and honor when Jesus Christ is revealed (1 Pet. 1:3, 6-7, TNIV).

May you be built up in your most holy faith as you pray in union with the Holy Spirit (Jude 1:20, CJB).

25
Blessings for Wisdom, Knowledge & Discernment

*The fear of the Lord is the beginning of wisdom;
a good understanding have all those
who do His commandments.*
~ Psalm 111:10a (NASB) ~

*If any of you lacks wisdom, let him ask of God,
who gives to all liberally and without reproach,
and it will be given to him.*
~ James 1:5 (NKJV) ~

King Solomon prayed for and received wisdom, discernment and breadth of mind greater than any human being who has ever lived. The book of Proverbs extols the necessity and value of obtaining wisdom. As Jesus sent out His disciples, He told them He would give them, *"Utterance and wisdom which none of your opponents will be able to resist or refute"* (Luke 21:15, NASB). Paul told us Jesus *"became to us wisdom from God"* (1 Corinthians 1:30, NIV).

We cannot permit ourselves to believe we possess any wisdom, knowledge, or discernment apart from that which God gives us. These are gifts from the Lord. Therefore let us be faithful to bless others with God's impartation of these divine attributes.

May the Lord fill *you* with the Spirit of God – with skill, ability and knowledge *concerning everything He has called you to do* (Exod. 31:3, NIV).

May the Lord endow you with the wisdom to carry out every assignment He has given you (Exod. 31:6, CJB).

May the Lord give you a heart to understand Him, eyes to see Him, and ears to hear Him (Deut. 29:4, CJB).

May the Lord give you wisdom and understanding so you will be able to obey the teachings of the Lord your God (1 Chron. 22:12, NCV).

May you think about what you are doing, not merely by human standards, but on behalf of the Lord who is with you when you do it (2 Chron. 19:6, CJB).

May you know that the Lord is God (2 Chron. 33:13, KJV).

May you *have the discernment and the willpower* to distinguish between the holy and the common, between the unclean and the clean (Lev. 10:10, NIV).

May the perfect law of the Lord restore your soul; the testimony of the Lord is sure…*His truth is certain. Therefore* may it make you wise (Ps. 19:7, NASB).

May you put your trust in the Lord: may He never allow you to be put to confusion (Ps. 71:1, KJV).

May the Lord direct you in the way of wisdom; may He lead you in upright paths. *As you allow Him to guide your* walk, your steps will not be impeded; and if you run, you will not stumble (Prov. 4:11-12, NASB).

May you give attention to *God's words of wisdom;* may you incline your ear to *the Lord's* sayings. Do not let them depart from your eyes; keep them in the midst of your heart; for they are life to those who find them, and health to all their flesh (Prov. 4:20-22, NKJV).

May you possess knowledge and discretion through wisdom *that comes from God* (Prov. 8:12, NIV).

May you find wisdom *and, in doing so,* find life and win approval from the Lord (Prov. 8:35, NLT).

May the Lord grant you the wisdom that comes with humility (Prov. 11:2, TNIV).

May you take pleasure in honest lips; may you value people who speak what is right (Prov. 16:13, TNIV).

May your house be built by wisdom and may understanding make it secure (Prov. 24:3, NIrV).

May you discover that wisdom excels folly as light excels darkness (Eccles. 2:13, NKJV).

May God give you wisdom and knowledge and joy; these things He gives to *the person* who is good in His sight (Eccles. 2:26, NKJV).

May wisdom make your face shine (Eccles. 8:1b, NKJV).

May the Spirit of the Lord rest on you – the Spirit of wisdom and understanding, the Spirit of counsel and might, the Spirit of knowledge and of the fear of the Lord (Isa. 11:2, NKJV).

May the Lord be your safety. He is full of salvation, wisdom, and knowledge. May respect for the Lord be your greatest treasure (Isa. 33:6, NCV).

May the Lord hear you when you call to Him and answer you. May He show you great and mighty things, which you do not know (Jer. 33:3, NKJV).

May you know the Lord is the one who answers your prayers and watches over you. He is like a green pine tree; your blessings come from Him. A wise person will know these things, and an understanding person will take them to heart (Hosea 14:8b-9a, NCV).

May God give you knowledge and skill in all learning and wisdom (Dan. 1:17a, KJV).

May God give you understanding in all visions and dreams (Dan. 1:17b, KJV).

May God make you wise and may you shine like the brightness of the sky (Dan. 12:3a, NIrV).

May you be blessed with ears that listen *and may you understand the Word of the Lord* (Mark 4:9, NIrV).

May you increase in wisdom and stature, and in favor with God and man (Luke 2:52, KJV).

May you *walk in* the grace God has given you in Christ Jesus. May you be made rich in every way, in all your speaking and in all your knowledge (1 Cor. 1:4-5, NCV).

May the source of your life be Christ Jesus, whom God has made our wisdom, our righteousness, our sanctification and our redemption (1 Cor. 1:30, RSV).

May the God of our Lord Jesus Christ, the Father of glory, give unto you the spirit of wisdom and revelation in the knowledge of Him (Eph. 1:17, KJV).

May the eyes of your understanding be enlightened so that you may know the hope of God's calling, *so that you may know* the riches of the glory of His inheritance, and *so that you may know* the exceeding greatness of His power toward *you as you* believe according to the working of His mighty power (Eph. 1:18-19, NKJV).

May you, being rooted and established in love, have power, together with all the saints, to grasp how wide and long and high and deep is the love of Christ, and to know this love that surpasses knowledge – and may you be filled to the measure of all the fullness of God (Eph. 3:17b-19, NIV).

May your love abound still more and more in real knowledge and all discernment, so that you may approve the things that are excellent, in order to be sincere and blameless until the day of Christ; having been filled with the fruit of righteousness which *comes* through Jesus Christ, to the glory and praise of God (Phil. 1:9-11, NASB).

May God fill you with the knowledge of His will through all the wisdom and understanding that the Spirit gives (Col. 1:9b, TNIV).

May you live a life worthy of the Lord and please Him in every way: bearing fruit in every good work and growing in the knowledge of God (Col. 1:10, TNIV).

May you *keep* growing in the special favor and knowledge of our Lord and Savior Jesus Christ (2 Pet. 3:18, NLT).

May you buy from the Lord gold refined in the fire (*things of enduring, eternal value*), that you may be rich;

and white garments (*the redemption of Jesus' blood that washes our sins away*), that you may be clothed, that the shame of your nakedness (*sin and guilt*) may not be revealed; and *may you* anoint your eyes with eye salve (*spiritual discernment*), that you may see (Rev. 3:18, NKJV).

26

Blessings to God

Hear, O Israel: The Lord our God is one Lord.
~ Deuteronomy 6:4 (KJV) ~

He said, "O Lord, the God of Israel,
there is no god like You in heaven or on earth,
keeping covenant and showing lovingkindness
to Your servants who walk before You
with all their heart."
~ 2 Chronicles 6:14 (NASB) ~

Our highest calling is to honor God. He is our Creator, Redeemer, Father, and Lord. Deuteronomy 10:8 says, "The Lord set apart the tribe of Levi to carry the ark of the covenant of the Lord, to stand before the Lord to minister and to pronounce blessings in His name" (NIV). It is a humble privilege, as priests, to return words of blessing to God from His own Word in worship to Him.

Blessed be the Lord who rescued the children of Israel from the Egyptians and from Pharaoh, who rescued His people from the harsh hand of the Egyptians (Exod. 18:10, CJB).

Blessed be the Lord, who has not left *us* without a kinsman-redeemer...*Christ the Lord*. May He become famous throughout *the earth* (Ruth 4:14b, NIV).

Blessed be my Rock! Let God be exalted, the Rock of my salvation (2 Sam. 22:47 & Ps. 18:46, NKJV).

Blessed be the Lord, who has given rest to His people Israel, according to all that He promised; not one word has failed of all His good promise, which He promised through Moses His servant (1 Kings 8:56, NASB).

Blessed be the Lord God of Israel from everlasting, and to everlasting. Amen, and Amen (Ps. 41:13, KJV).

Blessed are You, Lord God of Israel, our Father, forever and ever. Yours, O Lord, is the greatness, the power and the glory, the victory and the majesty; for all that is in heaven and in earth is Yours; Yours is the kingdom, O Lord, and You are exalted as head over all. Both riches and honor come from You, and You reign over all. In Your hand is power and might; in Your hand it is to make great and to give strength to all. Now therefore, our God, we thank You and praise Your glorious name (1 Chron. 29:10-13, NKJV).

Blessed be the Lord, God of our fathers. Are You not God in the heavens? And are You not ruler over all the kingdoms of the nations? Power and might are in Your hand so that no one can stand against You (2 Chron. 20:6, NASB).

Blessings to God

Blessed be the Lord, the God of our fathers, who *puts thoughts, ideas, and direction into* the king's heart, and has extended lovingkindness to His servants before *men, great and small* (Ezra 7:27-28a, NASB).

Bless the Lord our God forever and ever: and blessed be Thy glorious name which is exalted above all blessing and praise. Thou, even Thou, art Lord alone; Thou hast made heaven, the heaven of heavens, with all their host, the earth, and all things that are therein, the seas, and all that is therein, and Thou preservest them all; and the host of heaven worships Thee (Neh. 9:5-6, KJV).

I will bless the Lord, who hath given me counsel (Ps. 16:7, KJV).

Blessed be the Lord, because He has heard the voice of my supplications (Ps. 28:6, KJV).

Blessed be the Lord, for He has shown me His amazing grace (Ps. 31:21a, CJB).

Blessed be God, who has not turned away my prayer or His lovingkindness from me (Ps. 66:20, NASB).

Praise the Lord, God our Savior, who helps us every day. Our God is a God who saves us; the Lord God saves us from death (Ps. 68:19-20, NCV).

O God, You are more awesome than Your holy places. The God of Israel is He who gives strength and power to His people. Blessed be God (Ps. 68:35, NKJV).

Blessed be the Lord God, the God of Israel, who alone works wonders. And blessed be His glorious name forever; may the whole earth be filled with His glory. Amen and Amen (Ps. 72:18-19, KJV).

Bless the Lord, O my soul, and all that is within me, bless His holy name. Bless the Lord, O my soul, and forget not all His benefits (Ps. 103:1-2, KJV).

Bless the Lord, you His angels, who excel in strength, who do His Word, heeding the voice of His Word. Bless the Lord, all you His hosts, you ministers of His, who do His pleasure. Bless the Lord, all His works, in all places of His dominion. Bless the Lord, O my soul (Ps. 103:20-22, NKJV).

Blessed be the name of the Lord from this time forth and forevermore (Ps. 113:2, KJV).

Praise the Lord, my Rock, who trains me for war, who trains me for battle. He protects me like a strong, walled city, and He loves me. He is my defender and my Savior, my shield and my protection (Ps. 144:1-2a, NCV).

I will extol Thee, my God, O king; and I will bless Thy name forever and ever. Every day will I bless Thee and I will praise Thy name forever and ever. Great is the Lord, and greatly to be praised; and His greatness is unsearchable (Ps. 145:1-3, KJV).

Blessed be the name of God forever and ever, for wisdom and might are His. And He changes the times and the seasons; He removes kings and raises up kings; He gives wisdom to the wise and knowledge to those who have understanding. He reveals deep and secret things; He knows what is in the darkness, and light dwells with Him (Dan. 2:20-22, NKJV).

Blessed be the King who *is* eternal, imperishable, and invisible, the only God there is – let there be honor and glory to Him forever and ever (1 Tim. 1:17, CJB).

Blessed *be God*, the only Ruler, the King of all kings and the Lord of all lords. He is the only One who never dies. He lives in light so bright no one can go near it. No one has ever seen God, or can see Him. May honor and power belong to God forever. Amen (1 Tim. 6:15-16, NCV).

Blessed be the God and Father of our Lord Jesus Christ! By His great mercy we have been born anew to a living hope through the resurrection of Jesus Christ from the dead and to an inheritance which is imperishable, undefiled, and unfading, kept in heaven for us (1 Pet. 1:3-4, RSV).

Blessing and honor and glory and power be to Him who sits on the throne, and to the Lamb, forever and ever (Rev. 5:13, NKJV).

Blessing, and glory, and wisdom, and thanksgiving, and honor, and power, and might, be unto our God forever and ever. Amen (Rev. 7:12, KJV).

27
Blessings over Israel

And I will bless those who bless you,
and the one who curses you I will curse.
And in you all the families of the earth will be blessed.
~ Genesis 12:3 (NASB) ~

For you are a holy people to the Lord your God;
the Lord your God has chosen you
to be a people for Himself, a special treasure
above all the peoples on the face of the earth.
~ Deuteronomy 7:6 (NKJV) ~

There has been a glorious awakening in the Church over the past fifty years. Believers are embracing the Jewish roots of Christianity. This growing awareness is stirring our desire to embrace Israel as the root into which we have been grafted.

We are appreciating that Jesus was an observant Jew who studied the Torah and the Prophets. He was a Rabbi and he adhered to Jewish customs. We are grasping the implications of what it meant when the Apostles went to the Temple and when they observed the Biblical feasts.

We recognize through God's eternal commitment to Israel that His love endures forever. We have a better understanding of His grace, mercy, and forgiveness for *us* by studying His unwavering faithfulness to Israel.

If the Creator of the universe chose the children of Israel to be His people, then we must love and support them. We honor God by blessing Israel and in return, we are blessed.

May the Lord surely bless you and make your descendants as numerous as the stars in the sky and as the sand on the seashore (Gen. 22:17a, NIV).

May you and your descendants possess the cities of your enemies (Gen. 22:17b, CJB).

May all nations on earth be blessed *by you and your descendants* because you have obeyed *the Lord* (Gen. 22:18, NIV).

May God Almighty bless you and make you fruitful and multiply you that you may become a company of many peoples (Gen. 28:3, CJB).

May *the Lord* give you and your descendants the blessing given to Abraham, so that you may take possession of the land God gave to Abraham (Gen. 28:4, NIV).

May your pleas for deliverance rise up to God (Exod. 2:23b, NLT).

May God hear your groaning and remember His covenant with Abraham, Isaac, and Jacob (Exod. 2:24, CJB).

May God look on *you and have* concern for you (Exod. 2:25, NIV).

May the Lord pay close attention to you (Exod. 3:16, CJB).

May the Lord keep vigil for all the people of Israel through all their generations (Exod. 12:42b, CJB).

May the Lord be your healer (Exod. 15:26, CJB).

May the Lord *be your* Banner, *Jehovah Nissi* (Exod. 17:15, NIV).

May *the Lord* come to you and bless you wherever He causes His name to be honored (Exod. 20:24, NIV).

May *the Lord* send an angel ahead of you to guard you along *your* way and *may He* bring you to the place He has prepared *for you* (Exod. 23:20, NIV).

May you worship the Lord your God, and may His blessing be on your food and water. *May the Lord* take away sickness from among you (Exod. 23:25, NIV).

May the presence of the Lord go with you as a sign that you have found favor in His sight. This will be what distinguishes you from all the other peoples on earth (Exod. 33:15-16, CJB).

May the Lord bless you and keep you; may the Lord make His face shine upon you, and be gracious to you; may the Lord lift up His countenance upon you, and give you peace (Num. 6:24-26, NKJV).

May *the Divine Presence of the Lord be with Israel. May* the Lord rise up! May His enemies be scattered; may His foes flee before *Him* (Num. 10:35, NIV).

May you be holy because the Lord your God is holy (Lev. 11:45, 19:2, NIV).

May the *Lord* walk among you and be your God, and you will be His people (Lev. 26:12, NIV).

May the Lord, the God of your fathers, increase you a thousand-fold more than you are and bless you, just as He has promised you (Deut. 1:11, CJB).

May you *follow* the decrees and laws as the Lord God commanded *Moses*, so that you will show your wisdom and understanding to the nations who will hear about all these decrees and say, "Surely this great nation is a wise and understanding people." What other nation is so great as to have their gods near them the way the

Lord *your* God is near *you* whenever *you* pray to him (Deut. 4:5-7, NIV)?

May you *live as* a holy people to the Lord your God; the Lord your God has chosen you to be a people for Himself, a special treasure above all the peoples on the face of the earth (Deut. 7:6, NKJV).

As you keep and obey the commandments, laws, and rulings of Moses:

• May Adonai your God keep with you the covenant and mercy He swore to your ancestors (Deut. 7:12, CJB).

• May Adonai your God love you, bless you and increase your numbers (Deut. 7:13a, CJB).

• May Adonai your God bless the fruit of your body and the fruit of your ground, your grain, wine, olive oil and the young of your cattle and sheep, in the land He swore to your ancestors that He would give you (Deut. 7:13b, CJB).

• May you be blessed more than all other peoples (Deut. 7:14a, CJB).

• May there be no sterile male or female among you, and the same with your livestock (Deut. 7:14b, CJB).

• May Adonai remove all illness from you. May He not afflict you with any of Egypt's dreadful diseases, which you have known (Deut. 7:15, CJB).

May the eyes of the Lord your God always be upon the land He gave you to possess, from the beginning of the year to the end of the year, for it is a land the Lord your God cares for (Deut. 11:12, CJB).

May God give you rest from all your enemies around you so that you live in security (Deut. 12:10, NASB).

May the Lord your God bless you just as He promised you – you shall lend to many nations, but you shall not borrow; you shall reign over many nations, but they shall not reign over you (Deut. 15:6, NKJV).

May you give freely without begrudging it, and the Lord your God will bless you in everything you do (Deut. 15:10, NLT).

After you have brought the first fruits of the *harvest* which the Lord has given you, and you have set it before the Lord your God, and worshiped before the Lord your God, *may you then* rejoice in every good thing which the Lord your God has given to you and your house (Deut. 26:10a-11a, NKJV).

May the Lord look down from His holy habitation, from heaven and bless His people Israel, and the ground which He has given you, a land flowing with milk and honey, as He swore to your fathers (Deut. 26:15, NASB).

Now it shall be, if you diligently obey the Lord your God, being careful to do all His commandments which He commanded you, then the Lord your God will set you high above all the nations of the earth. All these blessings will come upon you and overtake you if you obey the Lord your God (Deut. 28:1-2, NASB):

- Blessed shall you be in the city, and blessed shall you be in the country (Deut. 28:3, NASB).
- Blessed shall be the offspring of your body and the produce of your ground and the offspring of your

- beasts, the increase of your herd and the young of your flock (Deut. 28:4, NASB).
- Blessed shall be your basket and your kneading bowl (Deut. 28:5, NASB).
- Blessed shall you be when you come in, and blessed shall you be when you go out (Deut. 28:6, NASB).
- May the Lord cause your enemies who rise up against you to be defeated before you; they will come out against you one way and will flee before you seven ways (Deut. 28:7, NASB).
- May the Lord command the blessing upon you in your barns and in all that you put your hand to, and may He bless you in the land which the Lord your God gave you (Deut. 28:8, NASB).
- May the Lord establish you as a holy people to Himself, as He swore to you, if you keep the commandments of the Lord your God and walk in His ways. *Therefore* all the peoples of the earth will see that you are called by the name of the Lord, and they will be afraid of you (Deut. 28:9-10 NASB).
- May the Lord make you abound in prosperity, in the offspring of your body and in the offspring of your beast and in the produce of your ground, in the land which the Lord swore to your fathers to give you (Deut. 28:11, NASB).
- May the Lord open for you His good storehouse, the heavens, to give rain to your land in its season and to bless all the work of your hand; and you shall lend to many nations, but you shall not borrow (Deut. 28:12, NASB).

- May the Lord make you the head and not the tail, and may you only be above, and may you not be underneath, if you listen to the commandments of the Lord your God, which the Lord charged you to observe carefully; do not turn aside from any of the words which *the Lord commanded Moses*, to the right or to the left, to go after other gods to serve them (Deut. 28:13-14, NASB).

May the Lord give you a heart to understand Him, eyes to see Him, and ears to hear Him (Deut. 29:4, CJB).

As the Lord commanded you *in the days of Moses*, may you love the Lord your God, to walk in His ways, and to keep His commands, decrees and laws; then you will live and increase, and the Lord your God will bless you in the land you possess (Deut. 30:16, NIV).

May the Lord protect you, care for you, and guard you like the pupil of His eye, as an eagle that stirs up her nest, hovers over her young, spreads out her wings, takes them, and carries them as she flies (Deut. 32:10b-11, CJB).

May you *embrace* the true love God has for you – all His holy ones are in His hand, sitting at His feet. May you receive His instruction, the Torah Moses commanded, as an inheritance for *your* community (Deut. 33:3-4, CJB).

May the Lord bless your land with wonderful dew from heaven, with water from the springs below, with the best fruits that the sun brings, and with the best fruits that the moon brings. Let the old mountains give the finest crops, and let the everlasting hills give the best fruits. May the full earth give the best fruits, and may the Lord who lived in the burning bush be pleased. May these blessings rest on your head (Deut. 33:13-16, NCV).

May you partake of the abundance of the seas and of treasures hidden in the sand (Deut. 33:19b, NKJV).

May you be satisfied with favor and full of the blessing of the Lord (Deut. 33:23a, NKJV).

May the bolts of your gates be of iron and bronze (*may your defenses be impenetrable*); may your strength match the length of your days (Deut. 33:25, NLT).

May you know there is none like the God of *Israel*, Who rides the heavens to your help, and through the skies in His majesty. The eternal God is a dwelling place, and underneath are the everlasting arms (Deut. 33:26-27, NASB).

May you be happy, oh Israel. Who is like you, a people saved by the Lord, your defender helping you and your sword of triumph? Your enemies will cringe before you, but you will trample down their high places (Deut. 33:29, CJB).

May the Lord hearken unto your voice and may He fight for Israel (Josh. 10:14, KJV).

May the Lord your God be with you as He was with your fathers: may He not leave you or forsake you (1 Kings 8:57, KJV).

May your house be like *the tribe of Judah* through the offspring which the Lord will give you (*has given you*) (Ruth 4:12b, NASB).

May God cause you to live in prosperity, and may your children inherit the Promised Land (Ps. 25:13, NLT).

May God save His people and bless His inheritance; May He shepherd them also and carry them forever (Ps. 28:9, NASB).

May the Lord give strength to His people; may the Lord bless His people with peace (Ps. 29:11, NKJV).

Blessed is the nation whose God is the Lord; and the people whom He hath chosen for His own inheritance (Ps. 33:12, KJV).

May you taste and see that the Lord is good: blessed is the man that trusteth in Him (Ps. 34:8, KJV).

May the Lord protect you and keep you alive, and you shall be called blessed upon the earth. May the Lord not give you over to the desire of your enemies (Ps. 41:2, NASB).

May God give you victory. You will succeed because of the Lord's mighty power; you will succeed because He favors you and smiles on you (Ps. 44:3, NLT).

May there be peace on the mountains and goodness on the hills for your people (Ps. 72:3, NCV).

May your people, Israel, respect *the Lord* as long as the sun shines and as long as the moon glows (Ps. 72:5, NCV).

Under the reign of the Lord of Hosts, may the righteous flourish and prosperity abound till the moon is no more. May He rule from sea to sea and from the Euphrates River to the ends of the earth (Ps. 72:7-8, TNIV).

May there be an abundance of grain in the land, all the way to the tops of the mountains. May your crops rustle like Lebanon. May your people blossom in the city like the grasses in the fields (Ps. 72:16, CJB).

We pray for the peace of Jerusalem; may they prosper who love you. May peace be within your walls and prosperity within your palaces (Ps. 122:6-7, NKJV).

As you trust in the Lord, may you be like Mount Zion, which cannot be moved but abides forever (Ps. 125:1, NASB).

May the Lord bless you from Zion. May you see Jerusalem prosper all the days of your life and may you live to see your children's children (Ps. 128:5, CJB).

The Lord hath chosen Zion; He hath desired it for His habitation. May He rest there forever: *in Zion* may He dwell; for He has desired it. May the Lord abundantly bless her provision: may He satisfy her poor with bread. May He also clothe her priests with salvation, and may her saints shout aloud for joy (Ps. 132:13-16, KJV).

May the Lord *who* made heaven and earth bless thee out of Zion (Ps. 134:3, KJV).

May your farms be filled with crops of every kind. May the flocks in your fields multiply by the thousands, even tens of thousands, and may your oxen be loaded down with produce. May there be no breached walls, no forced exile, and no cries of distress in your squares. Yes, happy are those who have it like this! Happy indeed are those whose God is the Lord (Ps. 144:13-15, NLT).

May God veil the sky with clouds above you and may He provide the earth with rain. May He cause grass to grow on the hills and may He give food to the animals, even to the young ravens when they cry (Ps. 147:8-9, CJB).

May the Lord reveal His Word to Jacob, His laws and decrees to Israel (Ps. 147:19, TNIV).

May Israel rejoice in Him that made him: let the children of Zion be joyful in their King. Let them praise His name in the dance: let them sing praises unto Him with the timbrel and harp. May the Lord take pleasure in His people: He will beautify the meek with salvation (Ps. 149:2-4, KJV).

May you not be afraid for the Lord is with you; may you not be dismayed for the Lord is your God. May He strengthen you, may He help you, and may He uphold you with His righteous right hand (Isa. 41:10, NKJV).

May the Lord pour water out on your thirsty land. May He make streams flow on your dry ground. May God pour out His Spirit on your children. May He pour out His blessing on their children after them. May they spring up like grass in a meadow and may they grow like poplar trees near flowing streams (Isa. 44:3-4, NIrV).

Even if a woman were to forget the child at her breast and not show pity on the child from her womb, the Lord would not forget you, *Israel*. God has engraved you on the palms of His hands, your walls are always before Him (Isa. 49:15-16, CJB).

May the Lord console those who mourn in Zion, to give them beauty for ashes, the oil of joy for mourning, the garment of praise for the spirit of heaviness; that they may be called trees of righteousness, the planting of the Lord, that He may be glorified (Isa. 61:3, NKJV).

For Zion's sake I will not keep silent, and for Jerusalem's sake I will not keep quiet, until her righteousness goes forth like brightness, and her salvation like a torch that is burning (Isa. 62:1, NKJV).

May the nations see your goodness, Jerusalem, and may all kings see your glory. May you have a new name, which the Lord Himself will give you (Isa. 62:2, NCV).

May Israel be a crown of splendor in the Lord's hand, a royal diadem in the hand of God (Isa. 62:3, TNIV).

May people no longer call Israel "Deserted." May they no longer name your land "Empty." Instead, you will be called "The One in Whom the Lord Delights." Your land will be named "The Married One." May the Lord take delight in you. May your land be like a bride. As a young man gets married to a young woman, your people will marry you. As a groom is happy with his bride, the Lord will be full of joy over you (Isa. 62:4-5, NIrV).

May the Lord appoint watchmen on your walls, O Jerusalem; all day and all night may they never keep silent (Isa. 62:6a, NASB).

May all who remind the Lord of their needs in prayer never be quiet. *May we* not stop praying to Him until He builds up Jerusalem and makes it a city all people will praise. The Lord has made a promise and by His power He will keep His promise. He said, "I will never again give your grain as food to your enemies. I will not let your enemies drink the new wine that you have worked to make. The person who gathers food will eat it, and He will praise the Lord. The person who gathers the grapes will drink the wine in the courts of my Temple" (Isa. 62:6b-9, NCV).

Indeed the Lord has proclaimed to the end of the world: "Say to the daughter of Zion, 'Surely your salvation is coming; behold, *the Lord's* reward is with Him, and His work before Him.'" (Isa. 62:11, NKJV).

May you be called "The Holy People," "The Redeemed of the Lord"; and may you be called "Sought Out," "A City Not Forsaken" (Isa. 62:12, NKJV).

May the Lord extend peace to Israel like a river and the wealth of nations like a flooding stream (Isa. 66:12a, NIV).

May you come home and sing songs of joy on the heights of Jerusalem (Jer. 31:12, NLT).

May God bring you health and healing. May He heal you and reveal to you an abundance of peace and truth (Jer. 33:6, NASB).

May God be your inheritance: God Himself is your possession (Ezek. 44:28, KJV).

May you pursue the knowledge of the Lord. His going forth is established as the morning; may He come to you like the rain, like the latter and former rain to the earth (Hosea 6:3, NKJV).

May the Lord be like dew to Israel. May Israel blossom like a lily and may he take root like the cedars of Lebanon. May his branches spread out, may his beauty be like an olive tree and may his fragrance be like the cedars of Lebanon (Hosea 14:5-6, CJB).

May the *children of Israel* return again to the safety of their land. May they flourish like grain and blossom like grapevines. May they be as fragrant as the wines of Lebanon (Hosea 14:7, NLT).

May you be wise and understand the things of the Lord; may you be discerning and know them. For the ways of the Lord are straight and the righteous walk in them (Hosea 14:9, CJB).

May you *tear* your heart and not your garments. May you return to the Lord your God, for He is gracious and compassionate, slow to anger and abounding in love, and He relents from sending calamity. God will repay you for the years the locusts have eaten. You will have plenty to eat, until you are full, and you will praise the name of the Lord your God, who has worked wonders for you (Joel 2:13, 25-26, NIV).

May the Lord plant *you* upon *your* land. "*You* shall no more be pulled up out of *your* land which I have given *you*," says the Lord your God (Amos 9:15, KJV).

May you look to the Lord and may you wait for the God of your salvation *knowing He* will hear you. Your enemy will not rejoice over you because when you fall, you will arise *with the help of almighty God, the Lord of Hosts*; when you sit in darkness, the Lord will be a light to you (Mic. 7:7-8, NKJV).

May the Lord, who is good, be *your* stronghold in the day of trouble; He knows those who trust in Him (Nah. 1:7, NKJV).

May you rejoice in the Lord and may you be joyful in God your Savior, *even* though the fig tree does not blossom and there be no fruit on the vines, *even though* the yield of the olive should fail and the fields produce no food, *even* though the flock *may* be cut off from the fold and there be no cattle in the stalls (Hab. 3:17-18, NASB).

May you rejoice in the Lord and may you take joy in the God of your salvation (Hab. 3:18, CJB).

May the sovereign Lord be your strength! May He make you as surefooted as a deer and may He bring you safely over the mountains (Hab. 3:19, NLT).

May the Lord your God, as a victorious warrior, *be* in your midst...*at all times...no matter where you may be.* He will *rejoice* over you with joy, He will be quiet in His love *for you*, He will rejoice over you with shouts of joy (Zeph. 3:17, NASB).

May you take courage, all you people still left in the Land *of Israel*. May you take courage and work, for *God* is with you, says the Lord Almighty. His Spirit remains among you, just as He promised when you came out of Egypt. So do not be afraid (Hag. 2:4-5, NLT).

Many peoples and powerful nations will come to Jerusalem to seek the Lord Almighty and to entreat Him. In those days, may ten men from all languages and nations take firm hold of the hem *of each* of *your* robes and say, "Let us go with you, because we have heard that God is with you" (Zech. 8:22-23, NIV).

As you bring your whole tithe into the storehouse that there may be food in the Lord's house, may God throw open the floodgates of heaven and pour out so much blessing that you will not have room enough for it. May He prevent pests from devouring your crops, and may He prevent the vines in your fields from not casting their fruit. May all the nations call you blessed, for yours will be a delightful land (Mal. 3:10-12, NIV).

Appendix A
Israel & the Church

Israel is the first and eternal covenant partner of God. This book espouses the Biblical interpretation of the Church as heir to God's eternal covenant *with* Israel *through* Jesus Christ, the Messiah. This appendix is an overview of the Biblical basis for my views on this important topic.

The Abrahamic Covenant

We first look at the origin of Israel as God's chosen people. It begins when the Lord appeared to Abram in Genesis and called him out from all the other peoples of the earth. *"Now the Lord said to Abram, 'Go forth from your country, and from your relatives and from your father's house, to the land which I will show you; and I will make you a great nation, and I will bless you, and make your name great; and so you shall be a blessing; and I will bless those who bless you, and the one who curses you I will curse. And in you all the families of the earth will be blessed'"* (Gen. 12:1-3, NASB).

Verse three also contains the important revelation that "<u>all</u> *the families of the earth*" would be blessed through Abram's ancestry. Later, the Scriptures illuminate our understanding that "all" have access to this blessing through the salvation that results from faith in Jesus as Savior. Furthermore, the concept of *"all the families of the earth"* would come to be understood as being wholly comprised of "Jews" *and* "Gentiles." "Jews" are the descendants of Israel (Abraham's grandson, Jacob) whereas all people groups who are not descendants of Israel are considered "Gentiles."

Continuing in chapter twelve of Genesis, God led Abram to the land of Canaan and promised to give the region to him and his descendants. God stipulated that He would give the promised land to Abram and his descendants *"forever"* in Genesis 13:15. In other words, the new homeland given to Abram and his descendants had a perpetual deed.

The Covenant Ritual

In Genesis 15, the Lord told Abram He would give him a son to be his heir. We also find the formal establishment of God's covenant with Abram. The covenant required the killing of clean animals requested by God and the separation of their carcasses through which God then passed. This "covenant cutting" ritual embodied Near Eastern culture that was well understood by Abram (Jer. 34:18). There was no misunderstanding that God obligated Himself to keep the terms of the covenant, regardless of what would happen on Abram's side of the relationship. Because God established the covenant, it was unconditional.

God next changed Abram's name to Abraham, in Genesis chapter 17, because He was making him *"the father of many nations"* (v.5, NKJV). He told him kings would descend from him and declared circumcision to be the sign of the covenant between them, *"and My covenant shall be in your flesh for an everlasting covenant"* (v.13, NKJV). The Lord announced that Sarah would bear him a son to be named Isaac and that He would establish His *"covenant with him for an everlasting covenant, and with his descendants after him"* (v.19, NKJV). Hence, the Lord declared His relationship with Abraham and his descendants to be one of a perpetual, everlasting nature; the covenant was to be eternal.

The Lord prophesied directly to Isaac that Messiah would come through his lineage in Genesis 26:4, *"I will multiply your descendants as the stars of heaven, and will give your descendants all these lands; and by your descendants all the nations of the earth shall be blessed"* (NASB).

In Genesis 28, the Lord appeared to Jacob, saying *"I am the Lord God of Abraham your father and the God of Isaac; the land on which you lie I will give to you and your descendants. Also your descendants shall be as the dust of the earth; you shall spread abroad to the west and the east, to the north and the south; and in you and in your seed all the families of the earth shall be blessed"* (v.13-14, NKJV). Here we see the covenant reaffirmed to Jacob.

God Remembered

Four hundred years later, God heard the groaning of the children of Israel to rescue them from slavery in Egypt. *"And God remembered His covenant with Abraham, Isaac, and Jacob."* The tenth plague God inflicted upon Egypt finally compelled Pharaoh to let His people go. In chapter 12 of Exodus, we observe the Lord kill all the firstborn in the land of Egypt except those of the Israelites, upon whose doorposts were sprinkled the blood of an unblemished lamb. *"Now this day will be a memorial to you, and you shall celebrate it as a feast to the Lord; throughout your generations you are to celebrate it as a permanent ordinance"* (Exod. 12:14, NASB). And so the Lord redeemed His people with the blood covering and brought them out of Egypt to begin their journey to the Promised Land.

Weeks later in the desert, after the giving of the law on Mt. Sinai, Moses *"took the book of the covenant, and read in the audience of the people: and they said, All that the Lord hath said will we do, and be obedient"* (Exod. 24:7, KJV). This important event marked the first time the entire nation of Israel acknowledged their covenant with God.

An Unconditional Covenant

From the remainder of Exodus through Deuteronomy, we find the giving and repeating of the Law (or more literally "teachings" or "Torah" in Hebrew) to His chosen people. We are struck by the repeated use of "if" statements describing what God's response would be to the Israelites' behavior. Despite God's numerous promises to reward their obedience with blessing and curse them with harsh judgments for their disobedience, He never once threatened to revoke His covenant with them. He did quite the contrary.

Forty years later, on the plains of Moab across the River Jordan from Jericho, Moses reviewed the entire the Torah with the young generation of Israelites who were about to inhabit the Promised Land. The Lord had all the people gathered to reaffirm His covenant with them, to establish for Himself a people as He swore to their ancestors, Abraham, Isaac, and Jacob. *"I make this covenant and this oath, not with you alone, but with him who stands here with us today before the Lord our God,* *as well as with him who is <u>not</u> here with us today"* (Deut. 29:14-15, NKJV).

The Hebrew word translated here as "not" is "ayin," from a primitive root word meaning "to be nothing" or "not exist"; a "non-entity." In other words, the covenant included those "not here," those who were not yet born...the generations to come!

Despite the golden calf, despite the high places of worship and sacrifices to foreign gods, despite Israel's failure to utterly destroy the nations God drove out before them, despite intermarrying with the inhabitants of the land, despite prostituting their sons and daughters...God always reminded them about their ultimate restoration. Why? Because, *"the Lord your God, He is God, the faithful God who keeps covenant and mercy for a thousand generations with those who love Him and keep His commandments"* (Deut. 7:9, NKJV). Love and obedience are not the conditions upon which the keeping of covenant depends; they are the behaviors of covenant keepers who are in covenant with God.

For the Sake of His Name

God acted justly and consistently in His harsh judgments upon the nation of Israel. He loved them, therefore He chastened them. In Deuteronomy 32, known as the "Song of Witness" or the "Farewell Song of Moses," we see God's resolve to spare Israel from destruction. *"I considered putting an end to them, erasing their memory from the human race; but I feared that their foes would mistakenly think, 'We ourselves accomplished this; the Lord had nothing to do with it'"* (Deut. 32:26-27, CJB). Therein resides the ultimate reason for God's unfailing devotion to His chosen people. It is to protect His reputation.

It is for the sake of His Name that He will not betray His covenant with Israel, regardless of their disobedience. God vowed to take vengeance on <u>His</u> foes and repay those who hate <u>Him</u> (v.40-42). Moses concludes his song, *"Sing out, you nations, about His people! For He will avenge the blood of His servants. He will render vengeance to His adversaries and make atonement for the land of His people"* (Deut. 32:43, CJB).

Just as Abraham recognized at the beginning, the prophets repeatedly spoke of God's enduring commitment to His chosen people. He used the prophets to speak assurance that His covenant would remain intact. Despite their apostasy, He always promised redemption and restoration to His people.

"Come now, and let us reason together, says the Lord, though your sins are as scarlet, they will be as white as snow; though they are red like crimson, they will be like wool" (Isa. 1:18, NASB).

"Behold, I will gather them out of all the lands to which I have driven them in My anger, in My wrath and in great indignation; and I will bring them back to this place and make them dwell in safety. They shall be My people, and I will be their God; and I will give them one heart and one way, that they may fear Me always, for their own good and for the good of their children after them. I will make an everlasting covenant with them that I will not turn away from them, to do them good; and I will put the fear of Me in their hearts so that they will not turn away from Me" (Jer. 32:37-40, NASB).

"And I will restore to you the years that the locust hath eaten, the cankerworm, and the caterpillar, and the palmerworm, my great army which I sent among you. And ye shall eat in plenty, and be satisfied, and praise the name of the Lord your God that hath dealt wondrously with you: and my people shall never be ashamed. And ye shall know that I am in the midst of Israel, and that I am the Lord your God, and none else: and my people shall never be ashamed" (Joel 2:25-27, KJV).

Enter, the Church

In the gospels, we read about the birth, death, burial, and resurrection of Jesus the Messiah and in the book of Acts, the establishment of "the Church." Jesus said, *"Don't misunderstand why I have come. I did not come to abolish the law of Moses or the writings of the prophets. No, I came to fulfill them"* (Matt. 5:17, NLT). The Apostles continued practicing their Judaism even though they had become believers in Jesus Christ and accepted Him as the true Messiah. Adherence to Jewish laws and customs was so intense among Jewish believers, controversy erupted in the early Church. At issue was the extent to which Gentile believers should be required to adopt the Jewish lifestyle.

The degree to which conversion to Christianity was synonymous with conversion to Judaism in the early Church is evident in Acts 15. Some Jews, acting independently from the main body of believers in Asia Minor, became confused in their understanding about assimilation of converted Gentiles into the Church. These "Judaizers" created a "different Gospel" by adding the requirement for circumcision in order to be saved.

Out of deep concern for this subversive challenge to the message of grace, Paul and Barnabas sought resolution with the Apostles and Elders in Jerusalem. Subsequently, the "Jerusalem Council" concluded *"we should not make it difficult* (that is, adding requirements like circumcision) *for the Gentiles who are turning to God"* (Acts 15:19, NIV). Instead, they wrote a letter telling them to *"abstain from food polluted by idols, from sexual immorality, from the meat of strangled animals and from blood"* (Acts 15:20, NIV). And so we see that a Jewish faction confronted the rights of Gentiles to become members in the Body of Christ without also conforming to traditional Judaism. It was Gentiles, not Jews, who were challenged. Jewish membership in the Church was a foregone conclusion.

One Body

The Apostle Paul taught that Gentile believers in Jesus Christ have been *"grafted in"* (Rom. 11:17). We, the Church, are supported by the root that sprung forth from the seed of Abraham. In other words, the Church did not uproot and replace the seed of Abraham. Paul also wrote, *"The Scripture, foreseeing that God would justify the Gentiles by faith, preached the gospel beforehand to Abraham, saying, 'All the nations will be blessed in you.' So then those who are of faith are blessed with Abraham, the believer"* (Gal. 3:8-9, NASB).

Truly, we have been blessed through the seed of Abraham. We have been given eternal life by *"Jesus the Messiah, the son of David, the son of Abraham"* (Matt. 1:1, NASB). *"If you belong to Christ, then you are Abraham's descendants, heirs according to promise"* (Gal. 3:29, NASB).

Paul described how Jews and Gentiles became "one man" through Jesus, *"But now in Christ Jesus you who formerly were far off have been brought near by the blood of Christ. For He Himself is our peace, who made both groups into one and broke down the barrier of the dividing wall"* (Eph. 2:13-14, NASB). Therefore, as members of the Body of Christ, we serve the God of Abraham, Isaac, and Jacob and we are partakers in the benefits and responsibilities of the covenant He made with them and their descendants.

Appendix B
Biblical Examples of Blessings

We find inspiration as we recognize the widespread impartation of blessings throughout the Scriptures. This section contains a sampling of blessings; it is not a comprehensive compilation. By examining these passages, we find blessings spoken by God the Father, by Jesus, by the Patriarchs, Prophets, and Apostles. The speaking of blessing can be observed from Genesis through Revelation.

We also note a progression that began with God directly blessing man, then God blessing through the Patriarchs, then God blessing through the priests. As believers in Christ, we, like the New Testament authors, are priests through whom God now blesses others.

Blessings By God the Father

When God blesses something it is permanently blessed. David said to the Lord *"For You, O Lord, have blessed, and it is blessed forever"* (1 Chron. 17:27b, NASB).

1. God blessed the newly created sea creatures and birds. *"And God blessed them, saying, 'Be fruitful and multiply, and fill the waters in the seas, and let birds multiply on the earth'"* (Gen. 1:22, NKJV).

2. God blessed newly created man. *"And God blessed them, and God said unto them, Be fruitful, and multiply, and replenish the earth, and subdue it: and have dominion*

over the fish of the sea, and over the fowl of the air, and over every living thing that moveth upon the earth" (Gen. 1:28, KJV).

3. God blessed the seventh day of the week, later to be identified as the Sabbath (or Shabbat, in Hebrew). *"God blessed the seventh day and separated it as holy; because on that day God rested from all His work which He created, so that it itself could produce"* (Gen. 2:3, CJB).

4. *"And God blessed Noah and his sons, and said to them, 'Be fruitful and multiply, and fill the earth'"* (Gen. 9:1, RSV).

5. God blessed Abram. *"Then the Lord told Abram, 'Leave your country, your relatives, and your father's house, and go to the land that I will show you. I will cause you to become the father of a great nation. I will bless you and make you famous, and I will make you a blessing to others. I will bless those who bless you and curse those who curse you. All the families of the earth will be blessed through you'"* (Gen. 12:1-3, NLT).

6. God blessed Sarai. *"God said unto Abraham, 'As for Sarai your wife, you are not to call her name Sarai (mockery); her name is to be Sarah (princess). I will bless her; moreover, I will give you a son by her. Truly I will bless her: she will be a mother of nations; kings of peoples will come from her'"* (Gen. 17:15-16, CJB).

7. God blessed Ishmael. *"And as for Ishmael, I have heard you. Behold, I have blessed him, and will make him fruitful, and will multiply him exceedingly. He shall beget twelve princes, and I will make him a great nation"* (Gen. 17:20, NKJV).

8. God blessed Isaac.

    "After Abraham's death, God blessed his son Isaac, who then lived near Beer Lahai Roi" (Gen. 25:11, NIV).

    "The Lord appeared to him and said, 'Do not go down to Egypt; stay in the land of which I shall tell you. Sojourn in this land and I will be with you and bless you, for to you and to your descendants I will give all these lands, and I will establish the oath which I swore to your father Abraham. I will multiply your descendants as the stars of heaven, and will give your descendants all these lands; and by your descendants all the nations of the earth shall be blessed; because Abraham obeyed Me and kept My charge, My commandments, My statutes and My laws'" (Gen. 26:2-5, NASB).

    "And the Lord appeared unto him the same night, and said, 'I am the God of Abraham thy father: fear not, for I am with thee, and will bless thee, and multiply thy seed for my servant Abraham's sake'" (Gen. 26:24, KJV).

9. The Lord blessed Jacob at Bethel, saying, *"I am the Lord, the God of Abraham your (grand)father and the God of Isaac. The land on which you are lying I will give to you and to your descendants. Your descendants will be as numerous as the grains of dust on the earth. You will expand to the west and to the east, to the north and to the south. By you and your descendants all the families of the earth will be blessed"* (Gen. 28:13-14, CJB).

Blessings by Old Testament "Visitors"

1. *"Then Melchizedek king of Salem brought out bread and wine; he was the priest of God Most High. And he blessed him and said: 'Blessed be Abram of God Most*

High, Possessor of heaven and earth; And blessed be God Most High, Who has delivered your enemies into your hand.' And he gave him a tithe of all" (Gen. 14:18-20, NKJV).

2. The Angel of the Lord blessed Abraham at Mt. Moriah, the place Abraham called "Jehovah Jireh" because it was there God provided a substitute sacrifice for Isaac. *"The angel of the Lord called to Abraham a second time out of heaven. He said, 'I have sworn by myself, says Adonai, that because you have done this, because you haven't withheld your son, your only son, I will most certainly bless you and I will most certainly increase your descendants to as many as there are stars in the sky or grains of sand on the seashore. Your descendants will possess the cities of their enemies, and by your descendants all the nations of the earth will be blessed, because you obeyed my order'"* (Gen. 22:15-18, CJB).

Blessings by Jesus, God the Son

1. Jesus gave the blessing at the Last Supper. *"Now as they were eating, Jesus took bread, and blessed, and broke it, and gave it to the disciples and said, 'Take, eat; this is my body'"* (Matt. 26:26, Mark 14:22, RSV).

2. After the Lord's disciples rebuked the crowd for bringing their children so that He might touch them, Jesus blessed the children. *"And He took them in His arms and began blessing them, laying His hands on them"* (Mark 10:16, NASB).

3. The Beatitudes. *"Looking at his disciples, he said: 'Blessed are you who are poor, for yours is the kingdom of God. Blessed are you who hunger now, for you will*

be satisfied. Blessed are you who weep now, for you will laugh. Blessed are you when men hate you, when they exclude you and insult you and reject your name as evil, because of the Son of Man. Rejoice in that day and leap for joy, because great is your reward in heaven. For that is how their fathers treated the prophets'" (Luke 6:20-23, NIV).

4. Before distributing the loaves and the fishes to feed the five thousand, Jesus spoke the blessing. *"And Jesus took the loaves, and when He had given thanks He distributed them to the disciples, and the disciples to those sitting down; and likewise of the fish, as much as they wanted"* (John 6:11, NKJV).

5. Jesus blessed His followers at His ascension. *"Then Jesus led them to Bethany, and lifting his hands to heaven, he blessed them. While he was blessing them, he left them and was taken up to heaven"* (Luke 24:50-51, NLT).

Blessings by the Saints of Scripture

1. Noah blessed God. *"Then he said, 'Blessed be the Lord, the God of Shem...'"* (Gen. 9:26, CJB).

2. Isaac blessed Jacob in place of Esau. *"May God give you of heaven's dew and of earth's richness – an abundance of grain and new wine"* (Gen. 27:28, NIV).

3. Isaac blessed Jacob as he sent him to the home of Rachel's father, Bethuel, to find a wife. *"May God Almighty bless you and give you many children. And may your descendants become a great assembly of nations! May God pass on to you and your descendants the blessings he promised to Abraham. May you own*

this land where we now are foreigners, for God gave it to Abraham" (Gen. 28:3-4, NLT).

4. Jacob blessed Joseph and his sons, Ephraim and Manasseh. *"And he blessed Joseph, and said, 'God, before whom my fathers Abraham and Isaac did walk, the God which fed me all my life long unto this day, The Angel which redeemed me from all evil, bless the lads; and let my name be named on them, and the name of my fathers Abraham and Isaac; and let them grow into a multitude in the midst of the earth'"* (Gen. 48:15-16, KJV).

   "So he blessed them that day, saying, 'By you Israel (the nation) will bless, saying, "May God make you as Ephraim and as Manasseh!"' And thus he set Ephraim before Manasseh" (Gen. 48:20, NKJV). Note: verse 20 is used in the traditional Sabbath eve blessings spoken over the sons in Jewish homes to this day.

5. Moses blessed the children of Israel upon completion of the wilderness tabernacle. *"The Israelites had done all the work just as the Lord had commanded Moses. Moses inspected the work and saw that they had done it just as the Lord had commanded. So Moses blessed them"* (Exod. 39:42-43, NIV).

6. God directed Aaron and his sons (through Moses) to impart blessings to the children of Israel. *"The Lord bless you and keep you; The Lord make His face shine upon you, And be gracious to you; The Lord lift up His countenance upon you, And give you peace. So they shall put My name on the children of Israel, and I will bless them"* (Num. 6:24-27, NKJV).

7. Moses imparted "The Solemn Blessing" to the children of Israel before they crossed the Jordan River to possess the promised land. It is so called because the blessings are juxtaposed with "The Solemn Dooms (Curses)" of Deuteronomy 27:15-26.

"Now it shall be, if you diligently obey the Lord your God, being careful to do all His commandments which I command you today, the Lord your God will set you high above all the nations of the earth. All these blessings will come upon you and overtake you if you obey the Lord your God: Blessed shall you be in the city, and blessed shall you be in the country. Blessed shall be the offspring of your body and the produce of your ground and the offspring of your beasts, the increase of your herd and the young of your flock. Blessed shall be your basket and your kneading bowl. Blessed shall you be when you come in, and blessed shall you be when you go out."

"The Lord shall cause your enemies who rise up against you to be defeated before you; they will come out against you one way and will flee before you seven ways. The Lord will command the blessing upon you in your barns and in all that you put your hand to, and He will bless you in the land which the Lord your God gives you. The Lord will establish you as a holy people to Himself, as He swore to you, if you keep the commandments of the Lord your God and walk in His ways. So all the peoples of the earth will see that you are called by the name of the Lord, and they will be afraid of you."

"The Lord will make you abound in prosperity, in the offspring of your body and in the offspring of your beast and in the produce of your ground, in the land which the

Lord swore to your fathers to give you. The Lord will open for you His good storehouse, the heavens, to give rain to your land in its season and to bless all the work of your hand; and you shall lend to many nations, but you shall not borrow. The Lord will make you the head and not the tail, and you only will be above, and you will not be underneath, if you listen to the commandments of the Lord your God, which I charge you today, to observe them carefully and do not turn aside from any of the words which I command you today, to the right or to the left, to go after other gods to serve them" (Deut. 28:1-14, NASB).

8. This is the blessing that Moses, the man of God, gave to the people of Israel before his death.

"The Lord came from Mount Sinai and dawned upon us from Mount Seir; He shone forth from Mount Paran and came from Meribah-kadesh with flaming fire at His right hand. Indeed, you love the people; all your holy ones are in your hands. They follow in your steps and accept your instruction. Moses charged us with the law, the special possession of the assembly of Israel. The Lord became king in Israel when the leaders of the people assembled, when the tribes of Israel gathered."

Moses said this about the tribe of Reuben: "Let the tribe of Reuben live and not die out, even though their tribe is small."

Moses said this about the tribe of Judah: "O Lord, hear the cry of Judah and bring them again to their people. Give them strength to defend their cause; help them against their enemies!"

Moses said this about the tribe of Levi: "O Lord, you have given the sacred lots to your faithful servants the Levites. You put them to the test at Massah and contended with them at the waters of Meribah. The Levites obeyed your word and guarded your covenant. They were more loyal to you than to their parents, relatives, and children. Now let them teach your regulations to Jacob; let them give your instructions to Israel. They will present incense before you and offer whole burnt offerings on the altar. Bless the Levites, O Lord, and accept all their work. Crush the loins of their enemies; strike down their foes so they never rise again."

Moses said this about the tribe of Benjamin: "The people of Benjamin are loved by the Lord and live in safety beside Him. He surrounds them continuously and preserves them from every harm."

Moses said this about the tribes of Joseph: "May their land be blessed by the Lord with the choice gift of rain from the heavens, and water from beneath the earth; with the riches that grow in the sun, and the bounty produced each month; with the finest crops of the ancient mountains, and the abundance from the everlasting hills; with the best gifts of the earth and its fullness, and the favor of the one who appeared in the burning bush. May these blessings rest on Joseph's head, crowning the brow of the prince among his brothers. Joseph has the strength and majesty of a young bull; his power is like the horns of a wild ox. He will gore distant nations, driving them to the ends of the earth. This is my blessing for the multitudes of Ephraim and the thousands of Manasseh."

Moses said this about the tribes of Zebulun and Issachar: "May the people of Zebulun prosper in their expeditions abroad. May the people of Issachar prosper at home in their tents. They summon the people to the mountain to offer proper sacrifices there. They benefit from the riches of the sea and the hidden treasures of the sand."

Moses said this about the tribe of Gad: "Blessed is the one who enlarges Gad's territory! Gad is poised there like a lion to tear off an arm or a head. The people of Gad took the best land for themselves; a leader's share was assigned to them. When the leaders of the people were assembled, they carried out the Lord's justice and obeyed his regulations for Israel."

Moses said this about the tribe of Dan: "Dan is a lion's cub, leaping out from Bashan."

Moses said this about the tribe of Naphtali: "O Naphtali, you are rich in favor and full of the Lord's blessings; may you possess the west and the south."

Moses said this about the tribe of Asher: "May Asher be blessed above other sons; may he be esteemed by his brothers; may he bathe his feet in olive oil. May the bolts of your gates be of iron and bronze; may your strength match the length of your days!"

"There is no one like the God of Israel. He rides across the heavens to help you, cross the skies in majestic splendor. The eternal God is your refuge, and His everlasting arms are under you. He thrusts out the enemy before you; it is He who cries, 'Destroy them!' So Israel will live in safety, prosperous Jacob in security, in a land of grain and wine, while the heavens drop down dew. How blessed you are, O Israel! Who else is like you, a people saved by the Lord? He is your protecting shield and your triumphant

Appendix B – Biblical Examples of Blessings

sword! Your enemies will bow low before you, and you will trample on their backs!" (Deut. 33:1-29, NLT).

9. Upon hearing the declaration of Boaz to redeem Ruth the Moabitess, as his wife, *"All the people and older leaders who were at the city gate said, 'We are witnesses. May the Lord make this woman, who is coming into your home, like Rachel and Leah, who had many children and built up the people of Israel. May you become powerful in the district of Ephrathah and famous in Bethlehem. As Tamar gave birth to Judah's son Perez, may the Lord give you many children through Ruth. May your family be great like his'"* (Ruth 4:11-12, NCV). *Note*: the middle portion of verse 11 is used in the traditional Sabbath eve blessings spoken over the daughters in Jewish homes to this day.

10. David blessed God.

    "I praise the Lord because He advises me. Even at night, I feel His leading. I keep the Lord before me always. Because He is close by my side, I will not be hurt. So I rejoice and am glad. Even my body has hope, because You will not leave me in the grave. You will not let your holy one rot. You will teach me how to live a holy life. Being with You will fill me with joy; at Your right hand I will find pleasure forever" (Ps. 16:7-11, NCV).

    "Blessed be the Lord, because He has heard the voice of my supplications" (Ps. 28:6, KJV).

    "I will bless the Lord at all times; His praise will always be in my mouth" (Ps. 34:1, CJB).

11. Solomon blessed God. *"Blessed be the Lord God, the God of Israel, who alone works wonders. And blessed be*

His glorious name forever; And may the whole earth be filled with His glory. Amen and Amen" (Ps. 72:18-19, KJV).

12. Daniel blessed God. *"Blessed be the name of God forever and ever, for wisdom and might are His. And He changes the times and the seasons; He removes kings and raises up kings; He gives wisdom to the wise and knowledge to those who have understanding. He reveals deep and secret things; He knows what is in the darkness, And light dwells with Him. I thank You and praise You, O God of my fathers; You have given me wisdom and might, and have now made known to me what we asked of You, for You have made known to us the king's demand"* (Dan. 2:20-23, NKJV).

13. Job blessed his children. *"After a cycle of banquets, Job would send for them to come and be consecrated; then he would get up early in the morning and offer burnt offerings for each of them, because Job said, 'My sons might have sinned and blasphemed God in their thoughts.' This is what Job did every time"* (Job 1:5, CJB).

14. Upon receiving the letter from King Artaxerxes of Persia, authorizing the return of the Israelites to Jerusalem for the temple restoration project, Ezra the scribe blessed the Lord. *"Blessed be the Lord, the God of our fathers..."* (Ezra 7:27, NASB).

15. After the rebuilding of the wall around Jerusalem was completed, Ezra took out the (Torah) scroll to read before the entire assembly. *"Ezra blessed the Lord, the great God, and all the people answered, 'Amen! Amen!'"* (Neh. 8:6, CJB).

16. The priests blessed the Lord and led all the people in blessing Him. *"Then the Levites, Jeshua, and Kadmiel, Bani, Hashabniah, Sherebiah, Hodijah, Shebaniah, and Pethahiah, said, Stand up and bless the Lord your God forever and ever: and blessed be thy glorious name, which is exalted above all blessing and praise. Thou, even thou, art Lord alone; thou hast made heaven, the heaven of heavens, with all their host, the earth, and all things that are therein, the seas, and all that is therein, and thou preservest them all..."* (Neh. 9:5-6, KJV).

17. Standing in the Temple courts, Simeon the righteous man blessed God as he held baby Jesus in his arms. *"Simeon took him in his arms and praised God, saying: 'Sovereign Lord, as you have promised, you now dismiss your servant in peace. For my eyes have seen your salvation, which you have prepared in the sight of all people, a light for revelation to the Gentiles and for glory to your people Israel'"* (Luke 2:28-32, NIV).

18. Simeon then blessed Joseph and Mary. *"Simeon blessed Joseph and Mary and said to the child's mother, Mary, 'This child will cause many in Israel to fall and to rise, he will become a sign whom people will speak against; moreover, a sword will pierce your own heart too. All this will happen in order to reveal many people's innermost thoughts'"* (Luke 2:34-35, CJB).

19. Paul the Apostle blessed God. *"Blessed be the God and Father of our Lord Jesus Christ, who hath blessed us with all spiritual blessings in heavenly places in Christ"* (Eph. 1:3, KJV).

20. Paul the Apostle concluded his epistles with blessings.

"The grace of our Lord Jesus Christ be with you" (Rom. 16:20b, RSV).

"May the grace of the Lord Jesus be with you" (1 Cor. 16:23, NLT).

"May the grace of the Lord Jesus Christ, and the love of God, and the fellowship of the Holy Spirit be with you all" (2 Cor. 13:14, NIV).

"The grace of the Lord Jesus Christ be with your spirit" (Gal. 6:18, Phil 4:23, Philem. 1:25, NASB).

"Peace and love with faith to you from God the Father and the Lord Jesus Christ. Grace to all of you who love our Lord Jesus Christ with love that never ends" (Eph. 6:23-24, NCV).

"Grace be with you" (Col. 4:18b, KJV).

"The grace of our Lord Jesus Christ be with you" (1 Thess. 5:28, NKJV).

"The grace of our Lord Jesus Christ be with you all" (2 Thess. 3:18, TNIV).

"May God's grace be with you" (1 Tim. 6:21b, NIrV).

"The Lord be with your spirit. Grace be with you" (2 Tim. 4:22, CJB).

"Grace be with you all" (Titus 3:15b, NASB).

21. The author of Hebrews concluded with a blessing. *"Grace be with you all"* (Heb. 13:25, NKJV).

22. The Apostle Peter concluded his epistles with blessings.

    "Peace to all of you who are in Christ" (1 Pet. 5:14b, NIV).

"But grow in grace, and in the knowledge of our Lord and Savior Jesus Christ. To him be glory both now and forever. Amen" (2 Pet. 3:18, KJV).

23. The Apostle John blessed Gaius. *"Beloved, I wish above all things that thou mayest prosper and be in health, even as thy soul prospereth"* (3 John 1:2, KJV).

24. The Apostle John blessed the reader of the book of Revelation. *"Blessed is he who reads and those who hear the words of this prophecy, and keep those things which are written in it; for the time is near"* (Rev. 1:3, NKJV).

25. The Apostle John concluded the book of Revelation with a blessing. *"The grace of the Lord Jesus be with all"* (Rev. 22:21, NCV).

The Book of Blessings Website

Please visit www.thebookofblessings.com regularly for more blessings and more about blessings.

Website Features

- A search function that allows you to search for blessings in two ways:
    - using key words contained in blessings,
    - using the names of occasions such as "birthday," "wedding," and "graduation."
- A blessing of the day to bless you!
- A *Discussion Forum* where you can share your experiences using the book to bless others. Please let us know if *The Book of Blessings* had an impact on you or on someone you blessed.
- A downloadable electronic version of the book.

You are welcome to contact Scott Osborne directly:
- Telephone: 614-560-0111
- Email: scott@thebookofblessings.com

Thank you for your support and for your interest!

Beloved, I wish above all things
that thou mayest prosper and be in health,
even as thy soul prospereth.
~ 3 John 1:2 (KJV) ~

Breinigsville, PA USA
03 November 2009
226950BV00002B/1/P